Performance Pay for Teachers

D0537377

The first widespread incentive pay scheme was initiated in UK schools in 2000. This book is the result of a research project monitoring the whole process for three years from its inception. The authors visited schools, observed lessons, and solicited the views and experiences of over 2,000 teachers and headteachers and what they found out is presented in this lively and accessible book. They include the views of teachers who were successful in crossing the threshold, those who weren't, and those who chose not to apply, and headteachers who had to make the decisions. There is an extensive analysis of performance management in schools. Pulling the information together the authors focus on the following themes:

- Headteachers' views and experiences of training
- The outcomes of pay decisions in their own school
- Teachers' and heads' relationships with external assessors
- Their hopes and fears for the future
- What teachers changed and did not change in their teaching as a result of performance management
- What means schools employed to further teachers' professional development.

This timely book is a useful resource for anyone involved in education, whether it be as a classroom teacher, headteacher, administrator or policy maker.

Ted Wragg is Emeritus Professor of Education at the School of Education and Lifelong Learning, Exeter University, where **Gill Haynes** and **Caroline Wragg** are Lecturers, and **Rosemary Chamberlin** is a Research Fellow.

Performance Pay for Teachers

The views and experiences of heads and teachers

E.C. Wragg, G.S. Haynes, C.M. Wragg, and R.P. Chamberlin

RoutledgeFalmer
Taylor & Francis Group

LONDON AND NEW YORK

First published 2004
by RoutledgeFalmer
11 New Fetter Lane, London EC4P 4EE

Simultaneously published in the USA and Canada
by RoutledgeFalmer
29 West 35th Street, New York, NY 10001

RoutledgeFalmer is an imprint of the Taylor & Francis Group

© 2004 E.C. Wragg, G.S. Haynes, C.M. Wragg, and
R.P. Chamberlin

Typeset in Sabon by
HWA Text and Data Management, Tunbridge Wells
Printed and bound in Great Britain by
MPG Books Ltd, Bodmin, Cornwall

British Library Cataloguing in Publication Data
A catalogue record for this book is available from the British Library

Library of Congress Cataloging in Publication Data
Performance pay for teachers : the views and experiences of heads
    and teachers / E.C. Wragg ... [et al.].
        p. cm.
Includes bibliographical references and index.
    1. Teachers–Salaries, etc.–Great Britain.   2. Merit pay–Great
    Britain.   3. Teacher effectiveness–Great Britain.   I. Wragg, E.C.
    (Edward Conrad)

    LB2844.G7P47 2004
    331.2´813711´009–dc22   2003025218

ISBN 0–415–32416–5
ISBN 0–415–32417–3

Contents

List of tables

Preface

Teachers in England and Wales have normally been paid according to a set of national scales, rather than differentially for their 'performance', though for many years additional salary was available to those who carried out extra duties. The very term 'payment by results', a nineteenth-century system for giving more money to those schools whose pupils could answer questions posed by visiting inspectors, has usually been regarded with opprobrium.

Towards the end of its first term of office, which ran from 1997 to 2001, the Labour government introduced a system of performance-related pay for teachers. It then continued the system during its second term. This was the first time such a widespread incentive pay scheme had been initiated in UK schools, so it was both controversial and contested.

The first stage of the process was that experienced teachers had to apply formally, and in writing, if they wished to progress beyond the normal salary scale and cross the *threshold* to a higher scale, thereby earning an additional payment of £2,000. The second stage was the introduction of *performance management*, which required schools, over a nine-month or eighteen-month cycle, to monitor and improve the quality of what teachers did and eventually to decide which teachers should progress even further up the higher pay scale.

The authors of this book monitored the whole process for three full years from its inception in 2000, as part of a research project funded by the Leverhulme Trust. All the studies were conducted in England, as Wales followed slightly different procedures. A wide range of research methods was employed, including two separate questionnaires to a national sample of over 1,000 headteachers, case studies of both primary and secondary schools, observation of lessons, analysis of documentation, and interviews with and questionnaires to 'successful' and 'unsuccessful' teachers, union officials and local authority officers. We carried out an extensive review of international research in the field and studied the application of performance pay in other professions and forms of employment.

This book describes what actually happened during a rarely researched process, as seen through the eyes of three major constituencies:

- *Senior professionals in the school* – there were two national surveys of 1,200 and 1,100 headteachers, and intensive interviews with a much smaller number, to elicit their views and experiences of threshold assessment and performance management.
- *Teachers* – teachers who were successful and were awarded additional pay were studied, as well as those who did not pass through the pay threshold and were not able to progress to higher scales.
- *Other agents and agencies* – teacher unions and local education authorities were not given a major role by the government, but they did actually play a part, so their views and experiences were also solicited.

In order to report, analyse, compare and contrast these manifold views and experiences, the book is divided into three main sections.

Part I   Performance-related pay

Chapter 1 describes the nature and implementation of performance-related pay in education and in different professional settings, and gives an account of how we set about investigating its introduction and application in schools in England. Chapter 2 reviews the relevant research in the field.

Part II   Threshold assessment

The first part of the process was for schools to identify those teachers who should cross the pay threshold and proceed to the upper pay scale. Chapter 3 recounts the views and experiences of the process as reported by over 1,200 headteachers in primary and secondary schools, while Chapter 4 explores success and failure through studies of hundreds of teachers who succeeded in crossing the threshold, failed in their attempt, or who decided not to apply. Chapter 5 gives the views of two groups operating at the edges of the performance related pay processes – teacher unions and local education authorities.

Part III   Performance management

In this section we report the second stage of the process, when headteachers were expected to manage the 'performance' of their colleagues, and also decide who should progress even further up the higher pay scale. Chapter 6 analyses the views and experiences of over 1,100 headteachers in primary and secondary schools. The views and experiences of teachers themselves are analysed in Chapter 7, while Chapter 8 reports five case studies of individual teachers who encounter varying circumstances and manifest different attitudes towards performance-related pay. Finally, Chapter 9 looks across the findings and discusses what might be extracted from them.

There is one small but significant clarification necessary of what may without it appear to be confusing. During the research project the ministry responsible for education was changed after Labour was re-elected to a second term of government in 2001. Up to that time the ministry was known as the Department for Education and Employment (DfEE). After 2001 it became the Department for Education and Skills (DfES).

Readers not familiar with the education system in England might like to know about a number of matters mentioned in the book. Schools are subject to regular inspections, every four or five years, by the Office for Standards in Education (Ofsted). There are statutory Standard Assessment Tests (SATs) for all children aged 7, 11 and 14. At the age of 16, pupils take the General Certificate of Secondary Education (GCSE) in several subjects, and at 17 and 18 the Advanced Supplementary (AS) and Advanced (A2) level, usually in three or four different subjects. The results of some of these tests are published in national or local league tables. These are ingredients of what is often called a 'high stakes' evaluation system, which forms an important backcloth to performance-related pay, of which the heads and teachers studied in this research are well aware.

This account of the introduction and implementation of performance-related pay over a three-year period documents a unique time in the educational history of England, during which every teacher who was eligible and who wished to apply for access to higher salary scales, was closely scrutinised. It tells the story of a huge experiment such as had not been conducted before in living memory. The results were both expected, and unexpected.

Acknowledgements

We should like to express our gratitude to the Leverhulme Trust for supporting the Teachers' Incentive Pay Project. We should also like to thank the many heads, teachers, union and local authority officers who participated in this research project for their interest and their co-operation.

Part I
Performance-related pay

1 Performance-related pay

Introduction

The concept of 'performance' does not always commend itself to teachers when applied to the job they do. It is a term more often associated with sport, industrial production, stage and arena appearances by actors or musicians, circus animals even. The word suggests that anyone giving a performance is probably in the limelight, showing off perhaps, not a notion with which quieter teachers readily identify. It also carries negative connotations, as in 'What a performance…', meaning a long-winded rigmarole, an unnecessary waste of time, a poor show. In an industrial context there is an assumption that performance can be measured fairly accurately, in terms of output, profits, the production of inert commodities. These factors can make the word seem too cold and dispassionate a description of the essentially human activity that teaching is thought to be.

The same reservations attach to associated terminology, such as 'performance indicators', favoured by economists and accountants in their quest for confirmation that something is working well, or that it can be regarded as a wise and effective investment of money. Teachers who take a holistic view of their work feel uneasy when it is atomised into separate elements to be measured, weighed and then ticked off, one at a time. The feeling is not unlike that of the German author Goethe, who described in a poem how he tried to discover why a dragonfly was so beautiful, only to find that it became a crumpled, dismembered heap in his hand. The secret of its beauty had been life itself.

In these circumstances the phrase 'performance-related pay' can arouse a similar negative reaction. Those who dislike their work being seen as a 'performance' are hardly likely to embrace enthusiastically the practice of offering teachers cash rewards according to their perceived quality. On the other hand, the idea of paying people more money, if they are thought to be doing their job especially well, has a commonsense appeal to the general public. Some heads and teachers are in favour of both principle and practice, as this research will show, arguing that it is just and proper to pay more to those who are working harder. Indeed, making additional payments to certain teachers, but not others, has been a feature of the salary and reward structure for the profession in many countries, but the word 'performance' has not always figured in the transactions, as they may have been paid extra for seniority, or for particular duties and responsibilities.

This book reports the findings of a three year research project, the Teachers' Incentive Pay Project (TIPP), funded by the Leverhulme Trust at the University of Exeter. The principal aim of the study was to investigate, at school, regional and national level, what happened when the United Kingdom introduced one of the largest and most widely spread performance-related pay schemes ever devised. All primary and secondary schools in England and Wales had to select those teachers who were regarded as the most competent and reward them with additional salary payments. Such a mass introduction of cash rewards, based on performance-related criteria, was novel in the UK, so we were in a unique position to study its genesis and effects, as the project began before the scheme was launched.

In order to 'improve' what they do, people must change. Nobody improves by staying exactly the same. Yet in the Leverhulme Appraisal Project (Wragg *et al.* 1996), we found that fewer than half the teachers studied said they had changed what they did as a result of appraisal. Classroom observations endorsed this finding. It was going to be interesting to discover whether the awarding of cash appeared to produce different results.

In the past there had been different types of incentive pay for the teaching profession in England and Wales, usually in the form of extra payment for additional responsibilities or duties. The introduction, in 1998, of the post of Advanced Skills Teacher, signalled a new style of government incentive to teachers to stay in the classroom, rather than seek extra pay outside it. The nationwide scheme launched in 2000 was a huge step beyond that, for it involved the vast majority of teachers, not just a select few.

The research programme studied a large national stratified random sample of primary and secondary schools, using a mixture of quantitative and qualitative methods, and undertook a smaller set of intensive case studies. The project fitted in well with several of our previous large-scale studies of a similar kind in recent years, looking at classroom skills (Wragg 1993), teacher appraisal (Wragg *et al.* 1996), factors influencing the effective teaching of literacy (Wragg *et al.* 1998) and teachers alleged to be incompetent (Wragg *et al.* 2000).

Background

How to improve the pay of classroom teachers in primary and secondary schools was part of a problem that faced the government in the late 1990s, when recruitment and retention had become an important matter. It was already known that almost half of the 400,000 teachers working in 24,000 primary and secondary schools would be aged over fifty by the middle of the first decade of the twenty-first century. Large numbers of teachers were leaving the profession before the age of retirement, making retention at least as serious an issue as recruitment. Part of the challenge was to find ways of preventing teachers having to become headteachers, or take other posts outside the classroom, in order to earn a higher salary.

In the United States Furtwengler (1994) identified three major promotional strategies or 'ladders' for classroom teachers. These were:

1 Performance-based ladders: Progression up a scale based on evidence of professional competence.
2 Job enlargement ladders: Progression based on extra responsibilities.
3 Professional development ladders: Progression based on completion of staff development activities, coursework, advanced degrees.

Traditionally schools in the United Kingdom had made use of Strategy 2. This was usually carried out through the payment of specified sums of money to teachers given additional responsibilities, like acting as head of department or subject co-ordinator, taking charge of special educational needs, or running the school library. Gradually, however, the emphasis had moved much more towards Strategy 1, with certain teachers regarded as especially competent being awarded a higher salary. The initiative begun in 1998, introducing the post of Advanced Skills Teacher, allowed schools to pay certain teachers a higher salary if they were deemed to be particularly good at their job and were willing to advise and support other teachers in the same or a different school.

The major Strategy 1 type of initiative to be sponsored by the government, however, was the introduction of a full-scale system of performance-related pay which was to be widely applied. Initially it was thought that perhaps half of classroom teachers would be paid higher salaries. In a 2000 document entitled *Performance Management Framework* (DfEE 2000b), the Department for Education and Employment proposed that there should be annual appraisals for teachers covering both pupil progress and personal development, with three to six targets being identified and regular monitoring of teachers' progress during each year. These annual reviews were then, in the words of the document, to 'inform' the awarding of extra salary by school governors.

From September 2000 schools were required to draw up a 'fair and open' policy involving all their teachers. Priorities and objectives had to be agreed, and between three and six 'challenging' but 'flexible' targets identified for each teacher, covering pupil progress and personal development. At the end of the year, teachers' performance was to be assessed and a decision would then be taken about whether they should progress further up the salary scale.

The research programme

The main general aim of the research was to focus on schools in England, during the critical three year period when the new systems were being introduced and implemented, and to find out, by observation, questionnaires and interviews, what different primary and secondary schools actually did to implement performance-related pay: how they drew up procedures and set targets; how they monitored them; what happened in lessons and what teachers appeared to do to meet their targets, or whether there seemed to be little change; which factors were thought to facilitate and which to hinder implementation; how decisions about pay were made in practice, including a specific analysis of the part played by pupil performance data; and finally what heads and teachers thought about the process and the outcomes in retrospect, in the light of their own experiences.

Within the main broad aim of the research there were several specific objectives. These included eliciting the processes and outcomes in schools as experienced directly by the people involved, like heads, teachers, union officials and local authority officers. The design, over the three-year period, employed a mixture of methods. Two large-scale questionnaire surveys of over 1,000 headteachers would explore their views and experiences at early and later stages of the implementation process, while intensive case studies over a two or three year period would assemble the picture in individual schools and classrooms. Thus the approach overall was to use both a 'long shot' and 'zoom' technique. A large national sample of schools responding to questionnaires gives the broader picture, while an in-depth study of schools and individual heads and teachers offers a set of intimate local insights and thus provides the local/national comparison framework.

There were many research questions. How would decisions be made in different schools? What sort of training would assessors receive? Would there be any significant differences in practice between the primary and secondary sectors? Would teachers change their styles and strategies? How would pupil 'progress' be assessed? What would be the impact on teachers who were successful, as well as on those who were unsuccessful? Would personal relationships within schools be affected? What would be the role of the external assessor, whose responsibility it was to check that headteachers were acting according to the principles and practices laid down in the procedures?

The measurement of pupil learning was one of the most controversial parts of the government's policy. A number of heads, teachers and their union representatives voiced opposition to this kind of evidence even being part of the process. The 2000 performance management framework document sent to schools, however, was not quite the crude mechanical 'payment by results' model that had been anticipated by some critics. It stated that it was important for teachers' targets to be 'based on pupils' prior attainment'. The document also said that team leaders, when making their assessment, should address 'factors outside a teacher's control [that] may affect the achievement of objectives'. This modified 'value added' approach is capable of many different interpretations, so that is why one objective of the research was to explore how pupil data were used.

The methodology followed closely that employed in our previous project, described below. Questionnaires were piloted extensively on samples similar to the constituency being polled. Interviews were recorded and transcribed whenever necessary. All four researchers have observed hundreds of lessons and trained together to high levels of agreement on quantified methodology, while on qualitative data a 'rate until agree' approach was used to resolve different interpretations.

Anonymity was guaranteed to everyone. Questionnaires were filled in anonymously, which may increase the likelihood of frank responses, but removes the opportunity to carry out a follow-up with the same sample. Headteachers were not told which members of staff were being studied and teachers did not know what their heads had said in interview. All names of individuals and schools in this book are invented, to protect the people concerned.

Part of the research strategy was to consider practice in other countries and indeed in other professions that make use of performance-related pay, as some have a long tradition of using it. The General Electric Company in the United States conducted a seminal study of its effects as early as the 1960s (Meyer *et al.* 1965), concluding that, among other findings, it was important to separate in time the act of appraisal and the awarding of a cash bonus or reward, otherwise the one interfered with the other. We looked at certain schemes in industry and the professions that appeared relevant to teaching, and reviewed practice internationally. In the United States, for example, several states have tried it, though some have discontinued it. Furtwengler (1994) documented the response of state governors after 1984, when Lamarr Alexander, governor of Alabama, declared that no teacher in the United States had ever been paid a cent more for teaching well. Despite many promises to the contrary, most governors did little beyond setting up a committee or a pilot study. By 1995 only five states were still running large-scale schemes, though others had changed their system to one where schools rather than teachers received additional cash.

In addition to the direct study of an incentive and reward scheme there were several important underlying issues, many of which were to do with the dynamics within a school, or the way that power was exercised, either by those who wielded it officially, or by those who wrested it. In our study of the competence of several hundred teachers (Wragg *et al.* 2000) we found that power and control over decisions could fluctuate from one party to another as time progressed and circumstances changed. Matters like decision-making about a group of teachers by their managers lie at the very heart of what happens in a professional community. The United Kingdom was introducing one of the most ambitious and far-reaching schemes of performance-related pay ever conceived in a climate of some reservation among teachers' unions and individual teachers and heads. It was an innovation that seemed likely to be of worldwide interest.

Teaching and teacher 'effectiveness'

The debate about teacher 'effectiveness' is central to the performance pay issue. Teaching can be an extraordinarily busy job, with thousands of interpersonal transactions taking place inside a week and as little as one second between them in which the teacher must make a decision (Wragg 1999). As a result teachers lay down *deep structures*, favoured styles and strategies which they can produce rapidly and modify according to the context in which they find themselves. Teachers with twenty years' experience have probably asked over a million questions, given several million pieces of information and explanation, and offered praise or reprimand on thousands of occasions. If one purpose of performance-related pay is to change behaviour, then there are many repeats and rehearsals to unscramble, the equivalent of trying to unpick the grooved swing of a seasoned professional golfer.

The notion of 'effectiveness' is by no means a clear and uncontested matter. Different criteria or measures may produce different candidates. In the nineteenth century, teacher training institutions were known as 'normal schools', on the grounds that there was a single agreed 'norm' of teaching (Rich 1933). The pluralism of the twentieth century led to a diversity of teaching styles and there was no clear research evidence that one approach was universally more effective than another, since context, subject matter, pupil ability and prior experience will often influence both process and outcome. Indeed large-scale summaries of the relationship between process and product in classrooms over many decades have often stated precisely that.

Barr (1961), summarising several hundred American studies, concluded that teachers who were preferred by administrators or by pupils were not necessarily those whose pupils did well on tests. Doyle (1978) observed that reviewers of research into teacher effectiveness had concluded, with remarkable regularity, that few consistent relationships between teacher variables and effectiveness criteria could be established. Even reviewers of the same studies have sometimes reached different conclusions about them, as Giaconia and Hedges (1985) pointed out in their synthesis of research findings on effectiveness.

A number of usually smaller scale analyses have sometimes found advantages for one style of teaching over another. Sometimes such findings can contradict each other. For example, Gage (1978 and 1985) cited studies that tended to show a superiority of 'traditional' over 'progressive' methods so far as basic skills in the early years of schooling were concerned, while Kulik *et al.* (1979) reported a meta-analysis of American studies of the Keller Plan, a form of teaching involving pupils completing individual assignments, which showed higher learning gains among Keller Plan pupils than in comparable control groups.

It is common in classroom observation studies, to try and link teaching strategies with outcomes. Freiberg and his co-workers (Freiberg 1983; Freiberg *et al.* 1990; Freiberg and Driscoll 1992; Freiberg *et al.* 1995) are amongst many who have studied the effects of a number of classroom processes thought to be associated with pupil learning. Where teachers consistently applied certain class management principles, like creating an orderly environment, varying their strategies, supporting a climate of pupil reflection, providing greater opportunities for pupil self-discipline, and establishing closer links with parents and the community, there was more likely to be significantly greater pupil progress in reading, writing and mathematics. There were also fewer pupil exclusions and disciplinary referrals.

The advantages reported in these smaller scale analyses, however, are often relatively slight, not strong enough to support the universal endorsement of one single style of teaching or the wholesale abandonment of another. As a consequence many teachers fashion their own unique approach to teaching. Performance-related pay procedures brought the assessment and identification of what different people regard as effective teaching into sharper focus.

Performance-related pay: a definition

Performance-related pay is normally defined as a reward for employees according to their perceived merit, rather than for their length of service, qualifications or other attributes. There are several ways of arranging this, not all of them relevant to a public sector profession such as teaching. In industry and commerce, piece-work and the distribution of equity and profit shares are commonplace, as is the allocation of one-off bonuses, often on the completion of a particular project, or in recognition of a specific contribution. Performance-related or 'merit' pay, once agreed, may become a regular part of an employee's salary and can therefore be taken into account for pension purposes.

Economists sometimes distinguish between the terms 'performance-related pay' and 'merit pay'. The former is used in situations where there are specific measurable outcomes, whereas 'merit pay' may be given for less easily measured behaviour. Performance-related pay is more common for manual workers and merit pay for non-manual and professional workers. Most writers do not distinguish between the terms and may use 'merit pay' if they are American, 'performance-related pay' if they are British.

According to Murlis (1992), performance-related pay which becomes part of the employee's salary can be organised in four ways:

1　Acceleration: Arrangements may be made for those perceived to be performing well to proceed more quickly up an incremental scale. This often occurs in unionised organisations, as it is compatible with a negotiated uniform salary structure, but it has two main drawbacks – good performers eventually get stuck on the top of the scale, and even poor performers will get there one day.
2　Flexible ceiling: The problems of acceleration are partially addressed by the second arrangement, whereby employees are paid between 80 per cent and 120 per cent of a midpoint, so that poor performers never

reach the top, although there still comes a time when good performers have nowhere further to go.

3   Group bonus: The third form of performance-related pay which, again, often occurs in unionised work places, is performance-related salary increases in addition to a cost of living increase for everyone.

4   Individual bonus: Finally there is the arrangement of giving increases only for personal performance, often within the range of 0 per cent–20 per cent, possibly at the discretion of the employee's manager.

The rationale for performance-related pay

The prime purposes of performance-related pay are often said to be to recruit, retain and motivate the workforce. This is based on the belief that high quality workers are attracted to an organisation where they believe their ability will be rewarded. The current workforce is given the message that good performers are valued, while poor performers are not. The prospect of earning more money is assumed to motivate workers to work harder and/or more effectively in future.

Performance-related pay has additional aims or perceived bonuses, one of which is to make employees more aware of, or more committed to, certain organisational goals. When people discover that certain skills or specific behaviour are rewarded in a performance-related pay system, they also learn what it is that their employer considers important. A list of merit pay criteria for a sales manager, for example, might include the requirement that the person concerned should have organised a sales conference for the sales team. This may signal various elements that the employer values, such as nurturing, supporting, instructing, or keeping up to date those over whom one is in charge. As Protsik (1996) says, the way an organisation pays, or as she puts it, 'compensates' its employees is strategic:

> Compensation ... serves more than the simple purpose of paying people for their time and hard work. Compensation systems communicate organizational desires to employees.
>
> (Protsik 1996: 266)

Other objectives of performance-related pay identified by Kessler and Purcell (1991) are:

* weakening the power of the unions by making individual rather than collective contracts;
* making managers responsible for taking decisions;
* giving better value for money;
* advertising the organisation's core values;
* changing the culture of the organisation.

The study of performance-related pay in the public sector by the Organisation for Economic Co-operation and Development (1993) also mentions:

- encouraging greater accountability;
- strengthening the relationship between individual job goals and organisational goals;
- giving managers greater flexibility;
- saving money by reducing automatic increments;
- enhancing job satisfaction.

Only the first of the ten criteria listed above, weakening the power of the unions, has not been an overt claim by proponents of performance-related pay as an anticipated benefit of its implementation for the teaching profession.

The history and evolution of performance-related pay

I cannot promise the House that this system will be an economical one and I cannot promise that it will be an efficient one, but I can promise that it shall be one or the other. If it is not cheap it shall be efficient; if it is not efficient it shall be cheap.
(Robert Lowe (later made Chancellor of the Exchequer by Gladstone), quoted by Bourne and MacArthur 1970: 20)

With these words, performance-related pay for teachers in England was introduced to the House of Commons in 1861. The implementation of it would cut the growing cost of education, it was believed, if teachers did not succeed, or at least raise standards of achievement if they did. The proposal was the idea of a commission into the state of popular education in England (The Newcastle Commission). It intended:

to institute a searching examination ... of every child in every school ... and to make the prospects and position of the teacher dependent, to a considerable extent, on the results of the examination.
(Bourne and MacArthur 1970: 20)

The notorious 'payment by results' system lasted for thirty years. During this time teachers spent a great deal of time preparing pupils for their test, and were confined to a narrow, boring curriculum. Many attempted to arrange the school intake, while some cheated, or ignored bright children so they could concentrate on drilling and beating the slower ones to ensure they would satisfy the all-powerful inspectors. Although these events took place over a hundred years ago, the experience had a lasting effect on folk memory, colouring their views and prejudicing teachers against performance-related pay in any form. Until the introduction of twenty-first century plans for *threshold assessment* (determining whether teachers should go through to a higher pay scale) and *performance management*, performance-related pay for classroom teachers in England had not been tried since the nineteenth century, though it had been in operation for headteachers since 1991.

Performance-related pay may have lain dormant for a century in Britain, but in the United States, where the idea of successful individuals receiving financial reward fits well with a market-orientated society, performance-related pay for teachers has rarely been off the agenda. In 1918, 48 per cent of school districts operated some form of merit pay, though the schemes were usually short-lived, and 'merit' often turned out in practice to involve being white and male. By the end of the 1920s the percentage of districts with merit pay had fallen to 18 per cent.

The reasons given for introducing merit pay in the US were similar to those set out in the UK: recruiting, retaining and motivating the workforce. There were also events, however, which promoted a perception of failing educational standards. Johnson (1984) states:

> In the 1920s and again in the 1960s, educators enthusiastically instituted merit pay plans throughout the country. Each time widespread public concern about the country's international standing, promoted in the first instance by World War 1 and in the second by the launching of Sputnik and the ensuing space race, fuelled merit pay plans. Many citizens were convinced that if schools were to prepare students to meet international challenges, they would have to become more rigorous, business-like places.
>
> (Johnson 1984: 175–6)

In the 1980s, *A Nation at Risk* (National Commission on Excellence in Education 1983), a critical report of America's education standards, prompted debate about teachers' pay. President Reagan (1983) contributed the view that teachers should be 'paid and promoted on the basis of their merit and competence' if schools were to improve. Enthusiasm for merit pay in the US – from administrators and the public if not from teachers – has ebbed and flowed since the mid-1950s. Although schemes varied across the country, there were some discernible trends, with earlier schemes favouring evaluations of teaching made by supervisors, either making subjective assessments or ticking lists of supposedly desirable teaching behaviour. These were widely criticised, for example by Darling-Hammond (1986) who claimed that ticklist evaluation 'exacerbates the tendency to think of teaching as an unvarying didactic exercise that is unresponsive to the characteristics of students or the nature of learning tasks' (p.535). Johnson (1984) argued that merit pay, which may be easy to organise in certain industries, is unsuitable in education because of the difficulties of measuring teacher effectiveness.

By the early 1970s the number of merit plans in existence had halved, down to 5.5 per cent of school districts, and most had not lasted long. According to Johnson (1984), a survey of plans by the Education Research Service in 1978 found that they had been dropped:

> for a wide range of technical, organisational, and financial reasons: difficulties in evaluating personnel, failure to apply criteria fairly, teacher and union opposition, poor morale, staff dissension and jealousy, failure of the plans to distinguish between merit and favouritism, failure of the plans to meet their objectives, changes in the school systems' leadership or philosophy, collective bargaining, funding shortages, overall expense of the programs, and recognition that the merit pay bonuses did not provide sufficient incentives to teachers. The problems were legion.
>
> (Johnson 1984: 180)

Despite this, in the 1980s merit pay was once more on the agenda, due, according to Johnson (1984), to concern about the decline of productivity in the US relative to Japan and other industrialised countries. This time, the financial incentives offered were often given for quantity rather than quality (Jacobson 1992), with bonuses given for extra work or good attendance. The problem was that, while subjective judgements were liable to bias and open to accusations of favouritism, supposedly objective judgements measured what was measurable and not necessarily what was important. Neither form of evaluation was usually based on the outcomes of teaching–pupil progress.

Despite criticism and problems, the interest in merit pay for teachers never died away in the US, especially in the poorer, southern states, and in the 1990s it was being discussed once again. Johnson (2000) believed that new and prospective teachers had different expectations of their career compared with those trained in the 1960s and might be more enthusiastic about a pay system which rewarded their performance. A variety of schemes was introduced, some of which will be examined in Chapter 2.

Performance-related pay for teachers has risen and fallen on the education agenda of other countries too. In Australia, where the states and territories run their own school systems, the state of Victoria abolished one system of assessing teachers in the late 1970s and early 1980s. In 1992 a new government came to power and introduced what was called the Performance Recognition Programme (PRP), which rewarded individual teachers.

According to Thompson:

> Performance-related pay has been a controversial issue in government schools in Victoria for half a decade. Apparently intended to reward those making a significant contribution to their schools and students, it has been rejected by those it was supposed to motivate.
>
> (Thompson 2001: 158)

Its acknowledged strengths were that it fostered reflection and discussion between teachers and school principals, encouraged staff to work towards the same goals and the professional portfolios that teachers kept were useful when they went for promotion. Its failings, however, were similar to those found in the US twenty years previously: underfunding, subjective judgements and excessive extra work.

Such divided experiences have produced a number of international contradictions. As one country discards its system, another embraces it exultantly. Australia and England moved in exactly opposite directions at the same time. In 1999 a Labour government was unexpectedly elected in Victoria. It proceeded to abolish the individual reward system, at the very moment when it was being introduced by a Labour government in England (Thompson 2001).

Performance-related pay schemes in different countries have elements in common. Often there is a clear list of professional standards that teachers are expected to reach, usually divided into those expected of teachers at different stages of their careers, what in New Zealand are called 'beginning', 'fully registered' and 'experienced' teachers. In New Zealand, as may happen elsewhere, teachers are assessed annually against the relevant standards. The school principal can then award or defer progression up the incremental scale. 'Beginning' and 'fully registered' teachers who have not met the required standards are given more time to achieve them before competency procedures are started, while 'experienced' teachers who fall short return to 'fully registered' status.

Often teachers themselves have no objections to the standards, recognising them as legitimate descriptions of what teachers should be and do. The problems are in attempting to prove that the targets have been met. Lindblad and Popkewitz (2001) found that teachers in England, Portugal, Spain, Finland, Sweden and Scotland said they were less able to help pupils having difficulties, because they felt obliged to target those who would, if given extra help, reach the expected level. They also reported that the necessary paperwork involved in the appraisal process took an unacceptable amount of time.

The problem of concentrating on pupils' test and exam results, while neglecting other less easily measurable targets, has been recognised, and in Scotland efforts have been made to overcome it by using other 'softer' measures, such as parents' and teachers' views, as well as test scores. Schools and teachers have been encouraged to carry out rigorous self-evaluation of their progress in the five national priority areas: achievement and attainment; framework for learning; inclusion and equality; values and citizenship; learning for life. There is still concern, however, that the more easily measurable areas may take precedence over the less quantifiable ones.

The process experienced by the teachers studied in this research project was similar to what happened elsewhere. They had to apply to cross a pay threshold by submitting a portfolio and laying out their achievements against five standards. Next they were required to set themselves objectives and discuss progress towards these with their team leader. They were following a familiar and predictable route travelled by many teachers in other countries during previous decades, with some echoes of a century earlier.

2 Research and practice

Is there any relationship between financial rewards and employees' behaviour? The assumption when performance-related pay is introduced is that there must be a link, or a series of connections, between pay and teaching quality. It is assumed that good performance can be identified, and that teachers will teach more effectively if offered financial incentives. If employees in general, and teachers in particular, do not respond as predicted, then the incentive of performance-related pay might be ineffective. As was pointed out in Chapter 1, research into effectiveness is not always straightforward. This chapter explores such evidence as there is from research studies and considers practice in different countries. We also refer to work in different fields of employment, as this is often of interest. The manufacture of inert goods and the education of children are not at all the same, however. In industrial production output and quality can often be measured easily, whereas in education such notions are usually far more problematic, so comparisons must be viewed with caution.

The key reasons for introducing performance-related pay in any organisation, as was said in Chapter 1, are generally said to be improving the motivation, recruitment and retention of staff. There are, however, other expected benefits, like making clear to employees what skills and behaviour the employer values and wishes to promote and reward. This is particularly relevant to performance-related pay and what is commonly called the 'performance management' of teachers, as such schemes are usually introduced in order to raise standards of pupil achievement in schools. The central idea is that if teachers could only teach better, their pupils would learn more.

What is required, therefore, is a means of changing teachers' behaviour, since no-one improves by behaving in exactly the same way. With many teachers engaging in 1,000 or so interpersonal exchanges in a single day, often with one second or less in which to make classroom decisions, as was stated in Chapter 1, the deep structures laid down over many years are not excised easily, and changes to longstanding habits may not necessarily be achieved by cash inducements and rewards.

Furthermore, research in the field faces the same criterion problems as research into effectiveness generally. For example: if teachers do appear to 'improve', however this is defined, are such improvements the result of cash inducements, or the many other influences on teachers' classroom behaviour? Unsurprisingly there is very little systematic enquiry into this particular issue. As a result of the contested nature of teachers' performance and its rewarding, the research findings and practices we describe below are often diffuse, certainly not always clear-cut and in one direction. They fall under headings like 'motivation', 'recruitment' and 'retention', and some investigators have been keen to show either the positive or negative effects of performance-related pay policies in such matters.

Motivation

Empirical studies of some non-teaching organisations which introduced performance-related pay sometimes show that it can have a motivational effect. Lazear (1999) studied a firm of car windscreen fitters over the nineteen months in which it changed its pay structure by switching to piece rates. Its output increased by 44 per cent, half of which was attributed to improved working by the existing staff and half to improved recruitment. In the field of horse racing Fernie and Metcalf (1996) found that jockeys performed better when paid according to results, than when paid under a 'retainer' system and because of this, over time, the retainer scheme became less popular. This example is not, perhaps, strictly relevant to teaching. The scheme is intended to produce winners, not to improve the standard of horsemanship generally and, however hard jockeys try, a horse race can have only one winner. Once all jockeys were paid according to their performance, the success of performance-related pay for some of them would probably diminish.

Murnane and Cohen (1986) counsel against using evidence from industrial settings to support the case in education. They claim that performance-related pay works best where there are clearly measurable outcomes and, although this may apply to fitting windscreens and racing horses, it is not true of teaching, unless pupils' formal test results become the sole criterion of success. As Murlis (1992) says:

> New systems need to match the culture and values of the organisation. For those in education, this means that the pay and performance management systems operated in industry cannot be translated wholesale. They must be modified, adapted, even rethought, to match the special demands of schools and other educational institutions.
>
> (Murlis 1992: 69)

As Johnson (1984) points out, teachers are not like manufacturers:

The quality and consistency of the raw materials of teachers' work – the children whom they teach – are beyond their control. Teachers are expected to do the best with what they are given; discards are not permitted.

(Johnson 1984: 182)

There are, however, other public sector jobs with hard to measure outcomes where performance-related pay has been introduced and its motivational effect observed. Marsden and Richardson (1994) studied the effects of the introduction of performance-related pay into the Inland Revenue and found that staff did not believe that their motivation had improved. Asked if performance-related pay had led them to change in line with a range of objectives, such as improve the quality or quantity of what they did, work harder or give sustained high performance, a large majority replied negatively. Marsden and Richardson concluded that:

The positive motivational effects of Performance Pay ... were at most very modest ... Even worse, there is clear evidence of some demotivation.

(Marsden and Richardson 1994: 253)

Similarly, Marsden and French's study of performance-related pay in public services (1998) found that most staff did not believe it had raised their own motivation, though about half of civil service and hospital line managers believed that it had raised productivity and, to a lesser extent, quality. Richardson (1999a), in his report commissioned by the National Union of Teachers (NUT), considered studies into the introduction of performance-related pay in local government (Heery 1996) and the National Health Service (NHS) (Dowling and Richardson 1997), which again rely on self-reported judgements about individual behaviour. While over half of the local government respondents said that performance-related pay had had an impact on their work behaviour, a large majority did not believe that they worked any harder. Amongst the NHS workers, just under 30 per cent agreed that performance-related pay had improved their motivation, but it was still a small percentage (12 per cent) that admitted to working harder.

When considering the finding that workers did not believe performance-related pay had motivated them, it should be remembered that the admission that one works harder for extra money is not easy to make, as it involves admitting that one could have worked harder previously, but chose not to. Indeed, it may be especially difficult for those involved in public service, rather than private industry. Even if *all* employees do not work harder, or more effectively, improving the performance of between 12 per cent and 30 per cent may be considered worthwhile, provided that the other 70 to 88 per cent are not demotivated and working less effectively.

In the 1960s, a study of employee motivation (Herzberg 1966) suggested that employees are influenced by two types of rewards, which he calls 'motivators' and 'hygiene factors'. 'Motivators' are *intrinsic* rewards such as recognition, responsibility, achievement and the actual work, while 'hygiene factors' are *extrinsic*. These make work less unpleasant than it otherwise would be, by providing good working conditions and salary. Herzberg argued that hygiene factors have little effect on increasing effort because they do not promote psychological growth and, from this, Jacobson (1992) deduces it would be more productive to try to improve the intrinsic rewards of teaching, such as recognising the value of teachers' work and increasing the time they are able to devote to the children in their classes.

Another 1960s model of employee motivation known as the Expectancy Theory was put forward by Vroom (1964). This states that prospective rewards will motivate employees only if they believe that (a) they can improve their performance by working harder, (b) if they do work harder there is a high probability they will be rewarded, and (c) if the thought of having more money appeals to them. Odden (2003) claims that the increasingly common knowledge and skills-based pay systems, which reward not for employees' years of service but for the relevant skills they display, draw from Vroom's Expectancy Theory. They seek to provide incentives to teachers to improve their teaching and motivate them to adopt successful teaching strategies.

Jacobson (1992), however, maintains that the relationship between teachers' efforts and performance or results is not straightforward and that the realisation that certain conditions, such as overcrowded classes and poor resources, were preventing teachers from gaining their anticipated performance-related rewards, might be demotivating. He also questions the extent to which teachers are motivated by money, whether in the form of performance-related pay or high salaries and additional payments, suggesting that 'people should not be expected to work hard for rewards they do not find especially attractive' (p.37).

The findings on the attraction of money for teachers are somewhat contradictory, or perhaps illustrative of the fact that teachers' motivations are not one-dimensional. Lortie (1975) suggested that the financial rewards of teaching were not as attractive as the opportunity to work with children and do a worthwhile job. Yet Jacobson (1995) found that teachers in the US did respond to financial incentives. Once they were part of a culture where extra money was paid for extra work, they sometimes demanded extra payment for activities such as attending school governors' meetings, which other governors did voluntarily. This may be resented, and illustrates, he considers, a dilemma, in that:

> school systems turn to monetary incentives to motivate teachers, yet they really don't want teachers who are primarily motivated by money.
> (Jacobson 1995: 30)

Research in the US by Heneman and Milanowski (1999) into newly introduced performance-related pay plans in Kentucky and Charlotte-Mecklenburg found that teachers generally valued their bonuses. Given seventeen outcomes of the scheme, the $1,000 bonus scored well for 'desirability', but Heneman and Milanowski were less sure about whether it actually motivated teachers, rather than just being a welcome extra. It should also be remembered that the teachers were asked to rate the various outcomes of the scheme according to desirability, but not asked about the desirability of the scheme itself.

Odden (2003) found that when performance management schemes related to pay were introduced in Iowa, Cincinnati and Philadelphia, the substantial increases they brought were viewed positively and thought to be worth the change in the evaluation system, though teachers in Cincinnati later voted to discontinue the scheme. Money, though it may be motivating in some circumstances, is not the only reward teachers value. Jacobson (1995) notes that in Canada, where teachers have had the opportunity to take unpaid leave since the 1970s, many do so, even at financial cost to themselves, because they prefer increased leisure or educational opportunities to more money.

Self-funded sabbaticals also formed part of the performance-related pay system adopted in 1992 by the state of Victoria, Australia (Thompson 2001) and discontinued just as a similar scheme was starting in England. It was originally suggested that teachers in England might also wish to take a salary cut or spread four years' salary over five years in order to have the fifth year off. This was criticised at the time as unlikely to be taken up widely and subsequently slipped off the agenda. The fact that the idea appears from time to time and place to place, however, suggests that the motivational power of money may not be as strong as advocates of performance-related pay believe. As Jacobson (1995) says:

> Those who advocate the use of monetary incentives in education believe that teachers presently have plenty of free time, and therefore additional time and effort to be purchased. But ... many teachers view time as a more attractive incentive than money.
>
> (Jacobson 1995: 33)

Recruitment

School districts in the US set their own wage rates, and teachers' salaries vary widely. This makes it possible to study the effect of differences in pay levels on recruitment, and even in the majority of districts which do not have performance-related pay, the effects of different monetary rewards may be observed. Jacobson (1995) studied districts of New York with different starting salaries and found that those offering more money than neighbouring districts were better able to attract applicants of high quality. Newly qualified teachers may respond to financial incentives. Alternatively, higher salaries may be affordable in the more affluent areas, so the issue is by no means clear-cut.

Richardson (1999a) argues that performance-related pay is less important in recruiting newly qualified teachers than starting salaries:

> Some may be attracted by the (uncertain) prospect of accelerated increments but the effect on their career choice now of moving on to the proposed new pay spine in 5–9 years' time looks rather small ... It is probably starting salaries that have a disproportionate influence on young teachers' career choices.
>
> (Richardson 1999a: 28)

Kyriacou and Coulthard's findings on that point (2000), however, cast some doubt on Richardson's claim. Asked to select various factors which might be important in the choice of career, their sample of students placed a good starting salary eighteenth out of 20 possible factors, with only 19 per cent of them saying that a good starting salary was 'very important' in their choice of career (and only 5 per cent thinking they would find it in teaching). The students were divided into three groups – those who already wanted to teach, those who definitely did not, and those who had considered teaching and might be encouraged to choose it as their career.

The factors the whole group identified as most likely to encourage them to teach were the long holidays, a wish to share their knowledge and the fact that they would not have to pay for a Postgraduate Certificate in Education (PGCE) course. They were influenced against teaching by the media image of teachers and the belief that they would have to deal with disruptive pupils, perform bureaucratic tasks, face external inspections and work in underfunded schools.

The 'undecided' group was then asked about policies which might encourage them to take up teaching, and it was at this point that 64 per cent selected improved starting salaries. At the top of this list (selected by 68 per cent) were improved resources for schools and higher salaries generally (65 per cent), while down the bottom (considered as 'definitely encouraging' by only 27 per cent) was performance-related pay. There may, of course, be a difference in what student teachers state when filling in a questionnaire from the comfort of an armchair, and how they eventually act when applying for a job.

While it is clear that salary has an effect on recruitment, Kyriacou and Coulthard's findings suggest that it is not paramount in the choice of teaching as a career. One of the supposed benefits of performance-related pay is that it attracts capable employees who like the idea of being able to earn bonuses based on their individual merit or to progress quickly up the incremental scale. There is little to show that this is yet the case in teaching.

Retention

Recruiting teachers is one thing, retaining them within the profession for several years is quite another. Murnane *et al.* (1991) found that in Michigan and North Carolina, where attempts were made to attract people to teaching and cut staff turnover, teachers who received $2,000 per annum more than the state average were half as likely to leave teaching after one year as those who received $2,000 less than average. This accords with the findings of Jacobson (1988), that the school districts which gave attractive salaries to teachers in mid-career were the ones with the lowest rates of turnover. He notes that this applied also to women, thus challenging the commonly held assumption that salary is of less importance to women. Chapman and Hutcheson (1982) and Goodlad (1983) also found that, although teachers might not expect large salaries early in their careers, eventually they became unhappy with their remuneration and this affected the decision of some not to remain in teaching.

The Organisation for Economic Co-operation and Development (OECD) (1993) examined many public service performance-related pay schemes but reported they provided little firm evidence about staff turnover. In the US, performance-related pay schemes were introduced in the 1980s into several naval research laboratories on an experimental basis, and these were then compared with similar laboratories without performance-related pay. Turnover amongst high performers at the demonstration laboratories was lower than at the control group and average salaries were higher.

When investigating the possible effects of performance-related pay on retention in the teaching profession, Richardson (1999a) considered the possibility that the expected decrease in turnover of teachers who receive performance-related awards would be offset by increased turnover of disaffected teachers who do not receive the awards. He also speculated that the pay increases for some will be met, not by new money from the treasury, but by lower increases for other teachers, thereby running the risk that overall turnover will increase. Since one of the most commonly stated aims of performance-related pay, however, is to encourage high performers to stay and poor performers to leave, this could be seen as a positive, rather than negative outcome, unless it results in an overall shortage of teachers.

Though retaining good teachers is an obvious goal for education authorities and departments of education everywhere, it may be that this is becoming less feasible, regardless of whether performance-related pay is introduced or not. Kerchner and Elwell (2000) argue that the career plans of today's US teachers may be very different from those of a previous generation, in a climate in which most of their contemporaries will change jobs several times.

Some evidence supporting this claim comes from Peske *et al.* (2000) who studied new teachers in Massachusetts and found that some of them were exploring whether they liked the job, rather than anticipating dedicating themselves to it for life. Others had taken up the job for altruistic motives, while another group was doing the job to subsidise activities which were more important to them, such as being a musician. Peske *et al.* say that the group they call 'explorers' stays in teaching if they find it interesting, rather than because of the pay they receive. Kerchner and Elwell (2000) found that 20 per cent of the graduates they studied who started teaching in 1993 left within three years. However, it was not evident that they left because of dissatisfaction with their salary. New teachers who did not have a proper teacher induction programme were more than twice as likely to leave as others. The same was the case for those dissatisfied with their school's environment and with pupil discipline. Wragg and Wragg (2002) studied a group of 334 postgraduate student teachers at the end of their training and found that working conditions were thought to be more important than salary.

As part of their study of teachers in Cincinnati, Heneman and Milanowski (2002) interviewed teachers who left the district ('movers') or gave up teaching ('leavers'). The teachers were given eighteen aspects of their job and asked which, if any, was a factor in their decision to leave, and which aspects caused them most dissatisfaction. For both groups, while the top reason to go was lack of student discipline, the second was Cincinnati's teacher evaluation process and this, mentioned by 78.4 per cent, scored highest as a cause of dissatisfaction. The evaluation system was an integral part of Cincinnati's performance management scheme, which was introduced to link teachers' pay to their performance in a range of standards. It would appear from this that, for many teachers, the prospect of a time-consuming, rigorous evaluation, even if linked to generous pay increases, was neither motivational nor conducive to retention. As Heneman and Milanowski say:

> We doubt there is another district in the county in which 50% of its exiting teachers mention their teacher evaluation system as a factor in their decision to leave.
>
> (Heneman and Milanowski 2002: 14)

The teachers who stayed in Cincinnati apparently did not appreciate the scheme either, as in May 2002, just before the scheme was due to be finally adopted, 96.3 per cent of its teachers voted against it and the plan was dropped.

Disadvantages of performance-related pay

Despite some evidence that performance-related pay may motivate employees to work harder or more productively, and in some circumstances may help to retain high quality staff, there is also evidence of disadvantages and failures. Sometimes the problems are that the scheme does not produce the hoped for benefits. It is frequently the case, however, that a performance-related pay system does not last long enough to be successful, so it is discontinued because it suffers from some of the unacceptable and undesirable side effects described below.

Neglect of unrewarded tasks

By rewarding particular aspects of a job, performance-related pay sends out messages about what is valued and the sort of behaviour that is desired. This is usually recognised as being an objective of performance-related pay, as it focuses employees' attention on what their employers think important. There is a danger, however, that it could be counter-productive if employees become so firmly fixed on hitting their measurable targets that other important elements of their jobs are ignored.

According to Kessler and Purcell (1991) this is one of the most frequently mentioned difficulties of performance-related pay and examples of the problem abound. Asch (1990) studied a Navy recruitment scheme, which set targets of how many recruits were wanted, and rewarded recruiters if they reached their targets by specific dates. Asch records how, immediately before the critical date, the number of recruits rose and their quality fell, suggesting that recruiters became less discriminating in response to their expected reward for meeting targets.

Heery's study (1996) of local authority employees found that 14 per cent admitted to concentrating on the measurable aspects of their job, while 10 per cent said they were less prepared to take on tasks not covered in their appraisal. This may not be a large proportion of the workforce, but it can still be an undesirable and potentially dysfunctional force. Richardson (1999a) noted that the proposed annual performance review for teachers set out by the UK government was expected to concentrate on three objectives. He observed:

> Unless some of these are set out in terms that are so general as to be vacuous there is a real danger that such a limit will mean that important parts of a teacher's normal duties will not be covered. If so it is very likely that some teachers will disregard some of their normal tasks.
>
> (Richardson 1999a: 29)

Murnane and Cohen (1986) identified what they called 'opportunistic behaviour' among some recipients of performance-related pay. They argued that workers ironing shirts and being paid piece-rates might neglect their machinery, while teachers might concentrate on raising pupils' test scores, but neglect their emotional needs or wider curricular goals. In some industries it is possible to overcome this problem by employing other workers to concentrate on those neglected tasks (e.g. to service the machinery), but it would not be easy to employ additional workers to instil into pupils a sense of responsibility or a distaste for taking drugs. Corbett and Wilson (1989) similarly expressed concern that teachers become overconcerned about test results:

The end result is that the major emphasis in the school becomes to improve the next set of test scores rather than some longer-term more general goal of improving student learning.

(Corbett and Wilson 1989: 36)

Concentrating on the pupils most likely to improve their test scores so as to meet the teachers' targets, while ignoring those who were already good enough or who would need a great deal of time and attention was one consequence of 'payment by results' in nineteenth-century England. Gramlich and Koshel (1975) found that it happened in the US when some private firms were rewarded on the basis of pupils' test scores for teaching reading in state schools.

Gillborn and Youdell (2000) found that this technique of 'borderlining' occurred in secondary schools where teachers had been set individual targets. They concentrated their efforts on those pupils at or just below the 'pass' mark at the expense of the high and low achievers. Indeed, 'booster' classes arranged for children about to take public examinations often focus on those whose level of attainment is just below the accepted standards. This is not simply a distortion which deprives some pupils of their share of teacher attention. Soucek (1995) argues that the emphasis on exam successes is at the expense of the intrinsic pleasure and satisfaction of learning, so that learning comes to be seen as guessing what it is the teacher wants.

In Scotland attempts were made to avoid over-emphasis on the measurable and to use means other than quantitative data to determine the quality of teachers and schools (Ozga 2003). Five national priorities in education were set out: achievement and attainment, framework for learning, inclusion and equality, values and citizenship, and learning for life. Schools were expected to evaluate their progress towards achieving targets in all five areas, not just in achievement and attainment, and indicators of success other than quantitative data are encouraged. Teachers too are expected to produce evidence such as feedback from parents and colleagues as well as pupils' exam results to show that they are working towards the priorities. Nevertheless, Ozga accepts that there is a danger that the easily measurable exam results will take priority.

Disagreement about goals

The problem that teachers might concentrate on certain aspects of their job and neglect others is related to questions about the aims of education and the role of teachers. With all the discussion about the merits of cash rewards and inducements, there has been little debate about the purposes of education. The assumption has been that everyone agrees about what a 'good' school is and does: its pupils are well-behaved, highly motivated and excel in examinations. The only problem, it is assumed, is how to get teachers to improve their teaching to achieve this ideal state of affairs.

In Cincinnati, however, local Montessori teachers (Pilcher 2000) had their own ideas of the 'good' school and the purposes of education. Their philosophy of education and teaching methods differed from those in mainstream schools and they were concerned that they might be judged according to goals they did not necessarily share. Johnson (1984) argues that without a clear consensus over what schools and teachers are aiming to do, merit pay, which rewards certain outcomes above others, is unsuitable:

> If schools do not define their goals, and if they pursue many goals simultaneously, expectations for teacher performance will be vague, muddled, or conflicting. No evaluation instrument, however carefully designed, can settle such issues.
>
> (Johnson 1984: 181)

A feature of many performance management systems in schools introduced in the 1990s and early twenty-first century, is that they set standards of what teachers were supposed to know and do at different stages of their careers. These were largely based on the framework for teaching set out by Charlotte Danielson (1996) and usually covered the knowledge, skills and attitudes that teachers were expected to demonstrate in various areas of their work, such as planning and preparation, classroom management, teaching, and involvement in wider professional activities. Broadly, teachers appear to agree with these descriptions of their role. In Cincinnati, Heneman and Milanowski (2002) found evidence of:

> teachers' widespread understanding and acceptance of the performance standard as highly job relevant and consistent with most teachers' conceptions of good practice. The standards can be considered as a competency model, and there was little disagreement among teachers as to the completeness and meaningfulness of the model.
>
> (Heneman and Milanowski 2002: 14)

In New Zealand the standards were negotiated between the government and teacher unions (O'Neill 2001), and so were thought to be acceptable by teachers as a reasonable description of their role. Hextall and Mahony (1999), however, criticise the English threshold assessment standards for presenting teaching as an individualistic activity, in which the teacher is seen as a technician with the knowledge and craft skills necessary to teach the National Curriculum, rather than as a critical professional. Disagreements about the role of the teacher and the purpose of education make the process of assessment problematic.

Lack of openness

Murnane and Cohen (1986) say that employees with performance-related pay will expect to have convincing reasons as to why some employees get more than others, and will want clear guidance about how they too can earn more money. Teaching, they argue, is not easy to evaluate in an unambiguous and uncontested manner, so one result may be that teachers are less willing to discuss problems with their headteacher, fearing that such discussions turn the 'coach' into the 'referee', who will rule against them. They also argue that, because of the imprecise nature of teaching, supervisors cannot always give a clear answer to teachers who want to know what they should do to earn the merit pay:

> Without an unequivocal answer to this second question, teachers may have little incentive to change their behavior in pursuit of higher income. What is worse, teachers may learn that concealing their problems and playing up to evaluators is what the organisation rewards – dramatically complicating managers' evaluation problem.
>
> (Murnane and Cohen 1986: 7)

The OECD (1993) investigation of performance-related pay for public sector managers identified another problem of lack of openness: the reporting of invalid data, or 'lying' as it is more commonly called. There are fears that, whenever targets are associated with cash rewards, people may invent evidence to show they have met the criteria.

Cost

Despite the assumption that performance-related pay schemes result in savings, because money does not have to be spread so widely, there are significant costs. Not only is there the actual money paid to the employees who are thought to deserve it, but also the cost of administration including monitoring, appraisal and performance management. On the subject of administration, Lipsky and Bacharach (1983) claim:

> the single salary schedule reduces uncertainty and unpredictability of future salary costs ... In terms of administrative cost *per se*, the simplicity of the single salary schedule makes it quite inexpensive to implement ... In comparison with other schemes (such as merit pay), few administrative personnel are needed to maintain the system. Widespread adoption of some alternative pay plan would probably require districts to hire additional administrators and would no doubt lead to a substantial restructuring of roles within the administration and possibly within the teaching staff itself.
>
> (Lipsky and Bacharach 1983: 7)

Thompson (2001) cited underfunding and the difficulties with budgeting as factors contributing to the failure of a performance-related pay scheme in the state of Victoria, Australia. Odden (2003) noted that in the US the performance-related pay systems in Cincinnati, Iowa and Philadelphia provided substantial increases in teachers' salaries, but said there was concern about whether the plans would be fully funded. Even if they were, he doubted whether other counties would follow the lead when they realised how much it would cost. In manufacturing industry costs can be passed on to customers and savings can be made if performance-related pay makes employees work faster and produce more. In teaching there is no such relationship between improved performance and increased profits, so fully funded performance-related pay schemes are expensive.

When Cincinnati's teachers voted to drop their performance-related pay scheme, the former associate superintendent of the Cincinnati Public Schools said that the evaluation scheme on which the performance-related pay was to have been based was very expensive and, if not linked to pay, might have to be dropped also (Delisio 2003). This suggests that there were planned savings to be made from linking teachers' pay to their evaluations, yet when the scheme was introduced, the emphasis shifted to the increases in salary that teachers could expect.

The president of the Cincinnati Federation of Teachers, Sue Taylor (Delisio 2003), said that teachers were not convinced the district had the resources to fund the scheme fully and, since the scheme offered more benefits to younger teachers, 'didn't feel comfortable leaving it as a legacy for future teachers'. A further criticism she made (Taylor 2002), was that:

> A handful of teachers would have received extremely large pay increases. Too many others could have seen reductions in pay based on evaluation standards and procedures on which they are just now being trained.
>
> (Taylor 2002)

Studying US school districts which dropped their merit pay plans, Cordes (1983) found that 17 per cent blamed financial problems, wholly or partially. Heywood (1992) drew attention to the difference between funding performance-related pay schemes in the public and private sectors. He cited the scheme organised for Her Majesty's Inspectorate (HMI) which was resented because funds were limited and inspectors who had earned additional pay did not receive the full amount. He assumed that, within teaching, money would always be in short supply and the number of bonuses given would be limited, which can cause resentment and rivalry. Hatry *et al.* (1994) studied eighteen US school districts from 1983 and found that few performance-related pay schemes were successful and lasting. They found that schemes were expensive if done well, but attempts to impose quotas on the number of teachers able to receive the awards, in order to limit costs, were destructive of teacher morale.

Protsik (1996) referred to a scheme in a district of Virginia, US in which bonuses were awarded to teachers who were rated 'skilful' or 'exemplary', but after five years the plan was suspended because of budget cuts. She claimed this was the common fate of performance-related pay plans in teaching, saying:

Most merit pay plans are discontinued within six years, largely due to problems of administration and personnel, collective bargaining, and budgetary shortfall.

(Protsik 1996: 274)

The OECD (1993) report also referred to funding problems in the public sector generally, as it is not so easy to make an accurate assessment of the cost-benefits of improved performance. Consequently, attention tends to be focused on the cost of the scheme, rather than on its more nebulous benefits. There is also the likelihood that:

> funding for performance pay schemes in the public sector may be vulnerable to budgetary cutbacks in times of economic constraint. This is a critical issue because the level and stability of funding for schemes are likely to have a major impact on the success of schemes.
>
> (OECD 1993: 62)

It is also critical because teachers' acceptance or rejection of a scheme may depend on their beliefs about its fairness, reliability and longevity. Marsden (2000) found that 82 per cent of the teachers he asked agreed with the statement that 'many excellent teachers will not pass the "threshold" because there is certain to be a quota on places available'. While teachers in England may not have followed the progress of performance-related pay schemes in the US, there was some scepticism about politicians' promises and their experience of funding problems made them suspect that at some stage the money would not be available to fund the scheme fully or fairly.

The money needed is not simply to meet the additional salary for good performers. Evaluating performance requires meetings, lesson observations and a variety of administrative tasks. Performing these incurs costs, either in paying supply teachers for cover of lessons and hiring additional administrative staff, or the cost of other worthwhile activities left undone. As Murnane and Cohen (1986: 3) observe: 'Monitoring the output or actions of individual workers is costly'. Evaluating a complex activity such as teaching is not cheap. Either it is done thoroughly, with a great deal of thought going into assessment criteria and the actual process, taking up considerable time of the headteacher and senior staff, or it is done perfunctorily, in which case it will be resented and may result in dissatisfaction and demotivation.

The cost of planning, meetings, observations, feedback and training is not only a financial one. Pupils cannot be left in an in-tray while teachers discuss their objectives or prepare their portfolios. Time is a precious commodity in schools, and performance management, whether or not it is linked to performance-related pay, takes a lot of everybody's time, whether assessor or assessed. Commenting on Victoria's discarded system, Thompson (2001) concluded: 'The system tended to generate a lot of additional work that was unwelcome' (p.172). Principals or their delegates had to carry out observations and assessments of their teachers and then, if it was decided that the teacher should either accelerate up the salary scale or have their next increment deferred, a panel had to meet to finalise the decision.

Cincinnati's evaluation was extremely comprehensive and time-consuming, though teachers did not have the same level of evaluation every year. Detailing the experience of one teacher, the *New York Times* (Rothstein 2001) reported:

> By year's end, Ms Staples, a 22-year veteran, will have been observed four times by a full-time evaluator and twice by her principal. The principal has also graded Ms Staples's lesson plans, examples of student work, letters to parents, her participation on faculty committees and whether she seeks added education to improve her teaching ... The district expected its 12 evaluators to assess about 700 of Cincinnati's 3,100 teachers this year, with time allotted for training, observations, written reports and meetings with principals to seek consensus on ratings.
>
> (Rothstein 2001: 9)

This does not mention the time Ms Staples and her colleagues would spend preparing their professional portfolios of evidence of their ability, or the extra time they would undoubtedly give to upgrading their lesson plans from note form to something more akin to a Booker Prize entry. It appears that the more a performance-related pay scheme seeks to be transparent, fair and comprehensive and to cover more than pupils' test scores, the more time it takes.

Demotivation for the unrewarded

The theory behind the motivational effects of performance-related pay is that the unrewarded will get the message that their performance is unsatisfactory and either improve or leave, both of which can be satisfactory outcomes from the perspective of the employer. Like many theories, however, it is too simple for complex reality, and in practice many employees who are satisfactory or better may be demotivated by schemes which do not benefit them.

In some schemes, in order to prevent spiralling costs or 'rating drift' as it is sometimes known, predetermined quotas are set, so that only a certain percentage of employees can receive bonuses or merit awards. The OECD (1993) reports that in a scheme in the UK civil service, introduced in 1987, a 25 per cent quota was set, later raised to 35 per cent. Thus 65 per cent of the staff, the vast majority of whom were appraised as being 'fully satisfactory', received no benefit. Dissatisfaction with this aspect of the scheme led to it being replaced by a new scheme with no quota. The OECD report states:

> If the aim of the performance pay scheme ... is to raise the performance of all managers then any assumptions regarding normal distributions of performance, and the resulting forced distributions of rewards, may be

dysfunctional. Forced distributions and quotas create 'winners' and 'losers' with the latter suffering some loss of self-esteem and becoming demotivated.

(OECD 1993: 66)

If everyone benefits, however, the purpose of the scheme may be undermined and costs can spiral. The OECD cites examples of plans where the majority of managers were rated as superior or outstanding, which, if the comparison was internal, is not logically possible. This corroborates findings on teachers' appraisals also, whether or not linked to pay awards. For example, in Baltimore, in 1983, 44.6 per cent of teachers were rated 'outstanding' (Digilio 1984), and Bridges (1992) cites examples of teachers diagnosed as extremely poor performers, who had been given good evaluations for many years in the hope of raising their esteem and encouraging them to live up to expectations. Thus, if everyone is rewarded, regardless of ability and achievement, the scheme is undermined, but if quotas are maintained these may demotivate the majority of satisfactory or good performers and also lead to the possibility of competitive attitudes replacing co-operation.

Competition instead of co-operation

There are several studies of the effects of performance-related pay on the level of co-operation in public services. Marsden and Richardson (1994) found that 26 per cent of their sample of Inland Revenue staff reported that performance-related pay had made them less willing to assist colleagues. A follow-up study by Marsden and French (1998) found that, despite management attempts to deal with some of the earlier disadvantages of the scheme, this percentage had risen to 63 per cent. The same survey found that 67 per cent agreed with the sentiment that performance-related pay discourages team-working, while the percentage who thought that it had caused jealousies had risen from 62 per cent to 86 per cent.

Heery (1996) studied employees from four local authorities, 18 per cent of whom felt that co-operation and teamwork had been damaged. Research into National Health Service managers by Dowling and Richardson (1997) found that, although 14 per cent thought they co-operated less or much less with their colleagues, 9 per cent thought they co-operated more or much more, and 77 per cent reported no change in co-operative behaviour. Similar findings emerge from a study of the Employment Service (Marsden and French 1998) in which 52 per cent of the sample said that staff were less willing to assist colleagues with their problems at work, and 78 per cent reported jealousies between staff.

Co-operation at work is required not only between equals, but also between employees and their managers. In the sample of local authority employees studied by Heery (1996), 16 per cent agreed that performance-related pay had eroded some of the trust between employee and manager, while Marsden and French (1998) found that 19 per cent of the NHS workers they surveyed admitted being less willing to co-operate with management. Marsden and French (1998) also looked at the problem from the perspective of NHS line managers, asking them about the attitudes of their subordinates, and 30 per cent reported that many members of staff were less willing to co-operate with management. It is interesting that a higher proportion of managers reported decreased co-operation between employees and management than did the employees themselves.

In his report for the NUT Richardson (1999b) concluded:

> Very many public sector workers see individual performance-related pay as leading to heightened tensions at work. It is seen to create jealousies amongst staff ... a sense of unfairness and ... to lead to a frequent loss of respect for management ... It strengthens a them-and-us attitude and reduces the sense of the team as a whole.
>
> (Richardson 1999b: 30)

Group payment schemes

In an attempt to avoid the problems that can occur from competition between staff, performance-related pay schemes may reward teams of employees rather than individuals. In order to address the criticism that merit pay is divisive and unfair, some school districts in the US experimented with schemes which reward the whole staff if certain goals are met. In a pilot scheme in Kentucky (Heneman and Milanowski 1999; Kelley 1998), schools were assessed according to 'accountability goals' and placed at one of five levels. Only those schools on the top level – the ones which had exceeded their goals – received a financial reward while those down in the bottom three categories had to produce 'transformation' plans, either on their own (category three) or with the help or under the control of a distinguished educator.

The rewarded schools were given a sum of money and staff voted whether to share it amongst themselves or spend it in some other way. Unsurprisingly, this caused some dissension, with disagreements about whether non-teaching staff should share the bonuses. Kentucky then joined some other states in rewarding the school with money to spend on extra equipment. Investigating the success of the scheme, Kelley (1998) found that teachers were motivated more by fear of the sanctions and the negative publicity that accompanied being categorised as a school in crisis, than they were by the expectation of money if they succeeded.

In Charlotte-Mecklenburg teachers were offered two levels of bonus if their schools reached a set of goals related to higher attainment, attendance and enrolment and lower dropout rates. There were two levels of bonus awards, with teachers in schools that succeeded in 75 to 100 per cent of the possible goals receiving bonuses of $1,000, while those in schools that were

60 to 74 per cent successful received $750. Continued failure meant that schools were designated 'priority schools' and given special help.

Heneman and Milanowski (1999) found that teachers in Kentucky and Charlotte-Mecklenburg liked their bonuses and felt that the scheme had other desirable outcomes, such as the satisfaction of achieving their goals and having this achievement recognised, co-operating with their colleagues and helping their students to achieve. There were disadvantages, however, including stress, adverse publicity and loss of professional pride if goals were not met, extra work, and less freedom to teach things unrelated to goals. Kentucky teachers also feared their loss of job security. Teachers' perception of the drawbacks to the scheme increased when the administration of the programme was felt to be unfair, as it frequently was, with some teachers believing their schools did not have a fair chance to achieve their goals. Heneman and Milanowski (1999) say that:

> Without careful planning, design, and administration of a SBPA (school-based performance award) program, and ensuring fairness as perceived by teachers, its high motivational potential will likely go unrealised.
>
> (Heneman and Milanowski 1999: 328)

Protsik (1996) argues that group-based performance pay plans help to focus teachers' efforts on working together to improve student learning. There is still some uncertainty, however, about the success of such group schemes. While group rewards are intended to promote a collaborative culture, they too have potential drawbacks. The extent to which merit pay can influence the content of lessons, for example, may be seen in reports of a school in North Carolina. A bonus of $1,500 was on offer for all teachers if their students' achievements improved, but as one of the targets for improvement was mathematics, teachers of all subjects focused heavily on that subject. According to the *New York Times* (Steinberg 2000):

> Several times a month, in preparation for a statewide math exam later this school year, the opening minutes of every 9th and 10th grade class ... are devoted to math, no matter whether the class is Latin, history or physical education. The math teachers give the gym instructors problems about batting averages, and ask the social studies teachers to work through equations related to the population of Japan. High school teachers sometimes isolate themselves in their classrooms, but the instructors ... in this suburb ... have been brought together, at least in part, in pursuit of a common goal: money.
>
> (Steinberg 2000: 20)

Many people may applaud such a Herculean cross-curricular effort, but the possibility exists that subjects such as physical education, or music, might be down-graded in importance, so that children are short-changed, missing out on a broad curriculum, as their teachers strive to secure the bonus that comes from good scores in mathematics tests. The morale of PE and music teachers might also be affected adversely.

Kelley (1998) analysed similarities between the Kentucky schools which achieved their goals and were rewarded. Her findings might fuel the worries of those concerned about the loss of teachers' autonomy and the imposition of particular goals. Describing the successful schools (successful, that is in achieving the goals set by the district authority) she said:

> All of these schools aligned their curriculum to the assessment instrument and/or to the state curriculum guides. All incorporated test-taking strategies into their regular curriculum ... they had direct contacts with the accountability program through professional teacher ties and current or past participation of teachers on state committees. As a result, these schools were more likely than others to know how to use and interpret the considerable amount of information issued by the state as a guide to help schools improve practice.
>
> (Kelley 1998: 309)

Fears of the return of 'teaching to the test' are not allayed by Kelley's findings. One of the aims of performance-related pay is to alert employees to those elements of their jobs that employers wish to emphasise, and this is as true of group schemes as it is of individual ones.

Success and failure

Although most performance-related pay schemes are short-lived, Murnane and Cohen (1986), in an attempt to find factors which enabled some districts to buck this trend, surveyed those with longer-lasting systems. They looked in vain for such districts in urban or disadvantaged areas, the very places most in need of the high-quality and well-motivated teachers that performance-related pay should encourage. Instead they found that schemes with greater longevity were usually located in small districts with homogenous populations, and most of these offered bonuses that were too modest to be motivational. Murnane and Cohen then selected six districts which did give larger differentials (up to $2,000 per annum in the 1980s) for closer scrutiny. These were all desirable neighbourhoods with above average pay scales and good working conditions and they also had the following in common:

- They gave extra pay for extra work, often also requiring teachers to produce evidence and documentation to prove their suitability.
- They strove to make all their teachers feel special and did not force teachers to participate in the merit pay scheme.
- The schemes were low-profile.

- Teachers were involved in planning the schemes, so there was general acceptance of the criteria for the awards and a feeling of ownership.

Murnane and Cohen concluded that these schemes did not really aspire to provide the benefits that merit pay is generally supposed to, like motivation, recruitment, retention and improving educational standards, but that they had other benefits. They supported good teachers and gave them the choice of whether to opt for a higher workload or more free time, and they encouraged teachers to be involved in evaluation. In a country where local democratic involvement in education is high, and often vociferous, they also helped to build community support for local schools and their teachers.

In order for performance-related pay schemes to work, Odden and Kelley (1997) argue that they need:

- involvement of all the key parties
- adequate funding
- training
- no quotas
- persistence.

Odden (2000) argues that in the past it had been difficult to fulfil these criteria, partly because of teachers' fears of subjective assessment and the lack of proper measures of pupils' achievement. He believes that, by the end of the twentieth century, this had changed, and the tools were in place for teachers to be paid for their knowledge and skills, rather than for their years of experience or their qualifications. The assessment tools aimed to assess teachers more objectively than principals' observations and more comprehensively than by pupils' test scores. Used in Ohio and Colorado, they tested teachers' knowledge, teaching practices and pedagogy. Such a knowledge and skills based system, backed up by accurate assessment, Odden believes, reinforces the elements that intrinsically motivate teachers, such as learning new teaching skills and being successful in helping pupils learn. To implement such a system, he says:

> A state or school district needs descriptions of the knowledge and skills desired as well as a process for assessing individual teachers according to the standards embedded in those descriptions. In 1990, such tools did not exist; today, there are several to choose from.
>
> (Odden 2000: 362)

It is not always wise to single out particularly successful performance-related pay schemes for detailed scrutiny and generalisation. By the time they have been analysed and publicised, they are likely to have changed or disappeared. An unexpected national or local election win may spell the end of performance-related pay, as happened in Victoria, Australia. A new union leader may be elected and teachers vote against the scheme, as happened in Cincinnati. A scheme may fail completely through lack of funding. Nevertheless, some schemes have worked through their initial problems and appear to have been accepted, usually by adhering to Odden's and Kelley's five requirements.

In Douglas County, Colorado, USA, for example, the involvement of key parties was achieved by having twenty teachers chosen by the teachers' union involved in the design of the performance-related pay scheme (Hinds 1999). Teachers in Douglas have several ways of earning bonuses above what is regarded as a reasonable base salary and they are rewarded for mastering skills identified by the district as desirable. To receive an annual increase, teachers have to be assessed by their school principal as 'proficient' or better, and this is based on observation rather than pupils' test scores. They can also earn more money by taking on extra tasks or get a bonus if they are considered 'outstanding'. In addition, there are group rewards for whole schools or departments who are involved in particular initiatives. Initial fears that the scheme would not be fair appeared to have been overcome when over three-quarters of Douglas's teachers received bonuses and found the scheme more acceptable.

The Douglas County scheme appears to have many of the criteria for success identified by both Murnane and Cohen (1986) and Odden and Kelley (1997): a good basic salary; extra money for extra work; teacher involvement and a feeling of ownership; no predetermined quotas; available training; full funding; and persistence. It also encouraged teachers to work together and thus avoided the pitfall of divisiveness. In Philadelphia, USA, teachers' involvement was secured by making the scheme voluntary, but with a bonus being given to all teachers who agreed to take part and additional rewards conditional on evaluations of their teaching ability.

Although the scheme was voluntary for serving teachers, it was compulsory for all new teachers, and so it was estimated that in seven or eight years nearly all the teaching force would be involved. The scheme was introduced in the face of opposition from the local teachers' union and was brought in before plans had been made about who would carry out the evaluations of teaching (Snyder 2000).

Philadelphia's scheme did not base its bonuses on the more contentious measure of student test scores, but some areas have done this. The Charlotte-Mecklenburg district gave bonuses to teachers who met annual improvement goals based on their pupils' test scores. Teachers in Florida were able to receive bonuses of up to 5 per cent of their salaries based on student performance, while in Maryland the cash went to the schools but not individual teachers.

Denver's pilot scheme also focused on student achievement (Janofsky 1999; Delisio 2003). A task force that included teachers, principals, education department officers and representatives of the community was set up to develop the scheme and monitor it up to the end of its trial period in June

2003. Teachers were promised that they would be given a vote on the final proposals in March 2004, and that, if 85 per cent of them agreed, the plan would be adopted. The pilot scheme operated in sixteen schools where teachers still received a basic salary but could gain bonuses for achieving objectives, agreed with the school principal, linked to improved student behaviour or attainment.

In October 2000, the president of the firm that introduced performance-related pay to the Colonial District, Montgomery County in 1998 said:

> Generally, there is enormous interest in trying to improve public education in America. It makes a lot of sense to use incentives to do that, since most people in the private sector already get paid that way.
>
> (Dean 2000: 3)

Colonial's plan gave bonuses to the top 20 per cent of teachers, thereby going against Odden and Kelley's injunction to avoid quotas, and was based on standardised test scores. In September 2001 teachers went on strike, claiming that the system had been forced on them, so the plan was dropped.

Conclusion

The track record of performance-related pay systems for teachers is not good. Many have failed because of the problems connected with evaluating accurately and uncontentiously the work that teachers do, since assessment was based either on the subjective opinion of principals, or the supposedly more objective judgements of ticklists and the pupils' test scores. Others have foundered because of funding problems or, according to Odden (2000), 'because merit pay is at odds with the team-based, collegial character of well-functioning schools' (p.362).

Nevertheless, many developed countries and American states have persevered towards a Utopian pay system which will reward good teachers, motivate others to improve and, most importantly, improve the standard of attainment of the pupils. Thirty states in the US have passed legislation requiring some type of performance pay for teachers.

Many of the plans introduced in the 1990s or early twenty-first century had significant similarities. They set out what teachers should know and do at various stages of their careers, similar to those in Danielson's framework (1996) and they required teachers to set objectives and undergo evaluation to demonstrate that these had been met. In New Zealand, beginning, fully registered or experienced teachers were appraised annually to demonstrate their ability in a range of Professional Standards similar to Danielson's model. In England and Wales there were specific expectations of newly qualified teachers and those who had completed their probationary year, plus opportunities for experienced teachers to cross a performance threshold and have access to higher salary levels, or to become 'advanced skills' teachers.

Other countries and states established ladders with more rungs. Cincinnati's plan was for teachers to progress through five levels, from 'apprentice' to 'accomplished teacher'. Their progress through the levels (and up the salary scale) would depend on an evaluation of performance in 16 standards in four areas: planning and preparation, creating a learning environment, teaching for learning, and professionalism. Time limits were set as to how long they could remain on the lower levels. Teachers in shortage subjects were able to progress more swiftly, an arrangement which prompts difficult questions about equity versus pragmatism and market forces.

There were regional and local differences, such as the need for New Zealand's teachers to understand the implications of the Treaty of Waitangi, which raised many issues about the position and rights of Maoris, but there were also many similarities which were not merely coincidental.

Consultation sometimes crossed international boundaries. Professor Odden, an American expert, was consulted by the Department for Education and Skills in London and, according to Lewis (2000), the British government then moved further and faster than that of the US. Writing in the US, she stated:

> None of the British reforms are unknown in this country. True, central-isation makes the task of instituting them comparatively easier in Britain, but schools with top performance are free of most supervision – other than a national assessment system. The major contrast, other than a willingness to link teacher performance to teacher pay, is a sense of urgency about the reforms. Professional development in Britain, for example, is expected to produce improvement within months, not the years predicted in the U.S.
>
> (Lewis 2000: 4)

It is these critical 'months' and the practices and aspirations associated with them which the Teachers' Incentive Pay Project studied. The story is of considerable interest across the world, for it was more intense and widespread than anything else being introduced at the time. It is to these events and the perceptions and experiences of those who participated in them, that we now turn in Part II.

Part II
Threshold assessment

3 Crossing the threshold

The views and experiences of headteachers

The introduction of performance-related pay occurred in two parts in England. The first involved making decisions about which teachers should be allowed to move on to a higher pay scale, beyond their current maximum. This phase was given the label *threshold assessment*. The second element was called *performance management*, and it required headteachers not only to manage the quality of teaching in their school, but to make further decisions about who should and who should not progress up this higher scale, known as the *upper pay spine*.

It might have been more logical, perhaps, to begin the process with a performance management programme and move on to a threshold assessment exercise later, on the grounds that once a scheme of nurturing teachers' professional skills is in place, decisions can then be made about who seems to be performing well enough to be paid more money. Political expediency, however, required the sequence to be played out in the reverse order.

Teachers were becoming increasingly disgruntled about their salaries and conditions of work. Furthermore, at the time performance-related pay was being introduced, there was a buoyant graduate labour market, so some schools were beginning to find difficulties attracting good quality applicants for vacant posts, especially in the more densely populated urban areas and in places where house prices were high. Consequently it became much more attractive, from a political standpoint, to be able to offer an initial £2,000 bonus quickly, rather than wait for a more long-winded general system of appraisal and management to take root. In the event, therefore, threshold assessment preceded performance management. We describe headteachers' attitudes to and experiences of the threshold assessment phase in this chapter, and our later study of their perceptions of performance management in Chapter 6.

Threshold assessment involved headteachers in an elaborate appraisal process in 2000, for they were the gatekeepers charged with running the exercise, subject to inspection by external assessors. The purpose of the threshold assessment procedure was to determine which of the teachers who were eligible for consideration, at or above point 9 in the existing pay scale, and who actually made an application (some elected not to, as we describe in Chapter 4) should be awarded a salary increase of £2,000 in this first round. Heads' experiences and views about the assessment are thus of considerable importance.

At the beginning of this research project we conducted extensive interviews with 31 primary and secondary headteachers. On the basis of these responses a questionnaire was then constructed to solicit the views and experiences of a large national sample of headteachers on several of the major features of threshold assessment, such as the training they had received, teachers' applications, time spent on the task, the role of external assessors, success rates in their school, and the reactions of those involved. As there are many more primary schools than secondary schools, it was sent to a stratified random sample of one in fourteen primary and middle school headteachers and one out of three secondary headteachers in schools in England.

Mailed questionnaires typically receive about a 10 per cent return, and it might have been lower, since many headteachers were boycotting paperwork at the time of our enquiry. However, the return rate was exceptionally high, some 53 per cent (1,225 out of 2,325) responding within four weeks, from schools in 150 different local education authorities. Responses were eventually received from 1,239 headteachers (56 per cent primary, 44 per cent secondary).

The questionnaire contained a mixture of open and closed questions. Qualitative analysis of people's spontaneous comments is extremely time-consuming, so we performed an intensive analysis, on a random sample of 500 questionnaires, of those sections where there were freehand responses to questions.

Training for headteachers

Two training days were available to headteachers, offered by the private company charged by the government with carrying it out. Heads were vitriolic in their condemnation of it, only one in eight describing it as 'good'. Some even walked out of the first session and several refused to return for the second day. A massive 57 per cent said they were 'very dissatisfied', probably the most negative reaction we have ever recorded from the various studies we have conducted over several years involving headteacher questionnaires. A further 20 per cent said that their training was merely 'adequate'.

Their comments were scathing, many describing it as the worst training they had ever attended on any subject. The trainers themselves appeared ill prepared. Indeed, many had been recruited from outside education. Heads said some had confessed openly that they knew little about school management, mechanically putting on numerous overhead transparencies for a few seconds, often with little understanding of the actual content. Instead of feeling they were respected partners, they saw themselves cast as operatives, so they were blistering in their condemnation:

It was the worst experience of my professional career – insulting, disorganised. The linesman at [the football ground where the training took place] was quite interesting – the training was not!

Poor, patronising and pedantic. Contradictory and written by people who have little understanding of schools.

Unutterably boring. No unscheduled questions could be answered and these were what I went for, since I can read the information as well as the trainer.

The training was not comprehensive enough. The trainers themselves lacked experience of educational management. The DfEE needs to question why it resorts to its list of multi-talented education consultants for whatever new initiative it wishes to deliver. The trainers' lack of experience and credibility needs to be set against the enormity of what we are being asked as headteachers.

If you are selling 'double glazing' that hardly anyone wants, that has been badly designed, that is incomplete and does not really work, then you are probably on a loser from the start – especially if you only heard about it the day before and still don't understand it yourself!

Only a small number of heads (about 7 per cent) felt that there had been an improvement by the second training day:

The first was poor. At the second, clearly, lessons had been learned.

First session dreadful (muddled, unclear); second session better – system and thoughts had been ironed out.

First day extremely controlled with no opportunity for professional discussion. Second half day much better – informative. Treated as a human being.

Many heads would have appreciated being briefed by fellow professionals who had themselves been thoroughly trained first. They felt that the conventions were being invented as time elapsed, rather than being thoroughly thought out in the first place. This led to confusion and different interpretations of what they should do, especially about the more complicated cases; one headteacher, among many, making the point forcibly:

Even after the second session it was clear that headteachers had differing attitudes towards the process and that uniformity/consistency was unobtainable. One key point was the issue of a significantly inadequate application from a good candidate, perhaps an over modest or self-deprecating person ('George' in the exemplar materials, if I recall correctly). From my group it was clear that some headteachers intended to treat such applications as 'not yet met' [the required standards] whereas others were prepared to 'fill in the gaps'.

Shifting ground rules

Government policy seemed to be changing during the training period and this generated considerable uncertainty. Trainers themselves appeared unsure about their central messages and this transmitted itself to the headteachers, adding to their concern. There was considerable confusion about the processes and conventions to be applied. The ground rules appeared to be shifting constantly, even between the first and second training days, on such fundamental issues as how many teachers ought to progress through the threshold. Assessors were given fresh instructions as training progressed, to reflect what appeared to be significant changes in policy.

This affected headteachers' confidence to proceed, especially when they were denied the opportunity to ask questions, or when the answers seemed uncertain and imprecise. Many said they had initially been given the impression that relatively few applications would be successful. Press reports began to suggest that half of all applicants would progress to the higher scale. But then the message from trainers switched dramatically, implying that most teachers would get the £2,000 bonus. In the event, as our research below shows, some 97 per cent of applicants crossed the threshold, but that was certainly not how it was being seen in the early stages:

> There were far too many questions which the leaders/advisors were unable to answer. Some answers had even changed overnight since their briefing meeting!

> At the first whole day training we were led to believe that only 'super' teachers were eligible for threshold payments, but at the second half day it was 'satisfactory and above'. Confusing!

The five standards of teaching

The training itself may have been confusing, but the standards against which teachers would be judged were actually named. Teachers' applications had to be evaluated on five sets of criteria:

1   knowledge and understanding
2   teaching and assessment
3   pupil progress
4   wider professional effectiveness
5   professional characteristics.

Heads found some of the standards more easy to judge than others and there were several differences between primary and secondary heads' responses. When heads were asked to rate, on a four point scale, the ease or difficulty they felt when making judgements about the five standards, most reported it to have been easy, rather than difficult. Table 3.1 shows their perception of the assessments.

Table 3.1 reveals that only about a quarter reported difficulty on four out of the five standards. It seemed a little harder to judge Standard 3, *Pupil Progress*, however, with over a third saying it was 'quite difficult' or 'very difficult'. This was for a variety of reasons, sometimes because more than one teacher taught the same class, as frequently happened in secondary schools, so picking out the contribution of just one of them was not always straightforward. Children with special educational needs usually learn more slowly than other pupils and some heads found it difficult to make a fair assessment of what might reasonably be expected. One primary head pointed out that pupil progress was sometimes in part a result of other interventions in the school, like booster classes, so everything was not necessarily reflective of what the class teacher had done. A secondary head was concerned that some teachers had just selected those groups which offered them the best evidence of progress, commenting 'What about other classes?!'

Paperwork and bureaucracy

Considerable paperwork was involved in processing applications and some heads were concerned about rewards going to those who were good at handling written documentation. Primary head comments on the pupil progress standard sometimes reflected a more holistic view of progress, less influenced by numerical data. This may, in part, be due to a lack of statistical information available to primary teachers in years when there were no national tests:

Table 3.1 Percentage of 1,239 headteachers saying how easy/difficult it was to assess each of the five standards

Standards	very easy %	quite easy %	quite difficult %	very difficult %
1. Knowledge and understanding	32	56	11	1
2. Teaching and assessment	29	56	14	1
3. Pupil progress	22	41	30	7
4. Wider professional effectiveness	26	51	21	2
5. Professional characteristics	26	48	22	4

There was insufficient data for individual teachers (e.g. Year 4 and Year 5) to support their applications regarding pupil progress. This is now being addressed so that future applications will be easier to complete.

This head's comment raises a particularly interesting issue. During the introduction of performance-related pay, sales of 'optional' tests (those for year groups that are not required to take them statutorily at the ages of 7, 11, 14 and 16) actually increased. Although some schools used them to help prepare for the compulsory tests, others gave them to pupils solely to provide data for teacher appraisal purposes.

Several heads referred to ambiguities in the evidence they should expect from teachers or were allowed to use and would have liked further guidance:

Evidence could be very selective. Therefore a teacher chose what to put down – did you judge only that or on everything you knew about them? In other words, were you judging the application or the applicant?

Some headteachers said judging the standards had been easy because of the way in which their teachers completed the application form:

My colleagues spent much of their summer half term completing their forms. I was very impressed with the detail and thoroughness.

Most of my staff worked hard to produce strong applications which were easy to assess.

These were generally schools where the head had also indicated that teachers had been given comprehensive training and support on how to complete their applications. This was, apparently, not the case in all schools:

Teachers do not have much guidance for completing the application forms. There is a need to make the criteria against which assessment is made very clear to teachers.

This may have been the reason why some teachers submitted what one head described as 'evidence which was sketchy or unclear'. Several head-teachers pointed out an important paradox: there were very capable teachers who submitted poor applications, and less effective teachers who submitted good ones:

Some of our most successful, as judged by Ofsted [the school inspection body], me, advisers, parents, pupils, did not do so well with the application form as some of our merely competent teachers.

Time

The amount of time heads said they spent on each application ranged from under an hour, in 11 per cent of cases, to over four hours, in 9 per cent of schools. Table 3.2 shows the range. Secondary school heads averaged about one and three-quarter hours per application; primary heads nearer two hours. The burden was taken almost entirely by headteachers themselves, only one in six (17 per cent) saying that it was shared with a senior colleague.

Many heads, both primary and secondary, resented the amount of time and bureaucracy involved with the threshold assessment procedure:

> No one made the days longer so that I could cope with 32 forms. The three who I judged 'not yet met' took a long time to consider, consult and complete. I had to get them right and they probably took 3 hours each at least.

> It was more a question of the process being very time consuming rather than easy/difficult.

Heads often preferred to use their knowledge of the staff in their school and felt that the bureaucracy was there to impress the external assessors, though they were not convinced that the latter would be any more enlightened about what were sometimes seen as vague and highly subjective guidelines:

> I am accustomed to judging the work of teachers by many informal observations and by seeing them at work. The judgement I had to make about the evidence was whether it would be strong enough to convince an outsider who had not observed their work.

> With the exception of teaching and assessment, they were not standards but guidelines, leaving a lot to judgement. I do not object to this as long as my judgement is respected. The standards on pupil progress were particularly vague.

Table 3.2 Time spent on each application by 1,239 headteachers

Time spent on each application	Percentage
Under 30 minutes	2
30–60 minutes	9
1 hour	33
2 hours	32
3 hours	15
4 or more hours	9

The problem was not in understanding the evidence but in understanding the standard. Teacher effectiveness is on a continuum and exactly where the threshold line is, is not clear even now. I only hope the threshold assessors have a clear idea.

Sharing the task

Heads often did not delegate any of the assessment to a senior colleague because they had been told not to, or because they thought it not fair on their overworked deputies, or on the staff who were being assessed. One said:

> Senior colleagues applied. I did not consider it advisable to delegate this work.

Another stated:

> I did all the assessment and verification. I spent a lot of time on the latter because I wanted to be able to show beyond doubt the accuracy/ rigour of the process.

Of the one in six heads (17 per cent) who did share the task, three-quarters were from the secondary sector:

> I dealt with half of the applicants and my deputies dealt with a quarter each. We all discussed all the applicants and I reviewed all the assessments made.

Although most heads did not *delegate* the assessment of applications to anyone, they did describe a variety of ways in which they used their deputies, and senior and some middle managers. Heads sought assistance for a variety of tasks. 'Verifying evidence' was the most frequently mentioned followed by 'helping staff'. Colleagues were asked to give second opinions and also for data analysis, lesson observation and to chase evidence:

> Deputies and two senior teachers were involved in initial assessment of those they line-managed.

> I asked a deputy to comment on my provisional judgements where I felt the standards may not have been met.

> I regularly discussed the process with the core leadership team but I made the judgements myself.

The teachers who applied

Most eligible teachers (on point 9 or beyond of the pay scale in operation at that time) in the schools studied did actually apply for the £2,000 payment. Table 3.3 shows that there were 25,851 teachers eligible to cross the pay threshold in our sample of 1,239 schools, and 88 per cent of those put in an application. In three-quarters (76 per cent) of schools, however, at least one teacher who was eligible did not apply. Other studies in this research project, reported in Chapter 4, show that people did not apply for different reasons, some refusing on principle, others being discouraged by the head or a senior member of staff.

'Success' rates

There were 22,131 successful and 633 unsuccessful applications. In nearly three-quarters of schools (71 per cent) every single teacher who applied was successful. These figures are not as straightforward as they look and are open to various interpretations. They can be presented in different percentage forms. The success rate in terms of *all eligible candidates* was 86 per cent. Taken as a percentage of *those who actually applied*, however, the success rate was 97 per cent.

It was difficult at this initial stage in the process to suggest what figure between 86 per cent and 97 per cent should be seen as a 'true' success rate, given that many teachers thought unlikely to succeed were discouraged from even applying. More information on this aspect emerged subsequently and will be reported in Chapter 4. Whichever way the figures are interpreted, however, it is certainly the case that the vast majority of eligible teachers did succeed in their applications.

Table 3.3 Teachers in the 1,239 schools who applied to cross the pay threshold

Number of teachers who were eligible to apply	25,851
Number of teachers who actually did apply	22,764 (88% of teachers eligible)
Number of teachers who were successful	22,131 (86% of teachers eligible, 97% of all teachers who applied)
Number of teachers who did not apply	3,087 (12% of teachers eligible)
Number of teachers who applied without success	633 (3% of all teachers who applied)
Schools where every applicant was successful	72%
Schools where not every eligible teacher applied	76%

Advising teachers

Some heads felt strongly it was not their role to advise teachers on whether they should apply. Indeed, they had been told they were not to intervene and only a few (6 per cent) said they had advised people not to apply:

> I am amazed you ask! It would be totally improper.

> I did not feel this was a suitable action to take.

> It would have been wholly inappropriate to do so.

Other heads said they had been warned by their union not to advise staff at all in this respect:

> Even had I thought it necessary, I was warned off by my professional association because of legal consequences.

Nonetheless the 6 per cent who did intervene, and this was twice as likely to occur in a secondary as in a primary school, said they had made sure that certain teachers were told, directly or indirectly, that their applications would *not* be supported:

> The Deputy Head who was given responsibility for doing preparation work with eligible staff had a number of conversations with several who did not choose subsequently to apply.

> This was done through intermediaries. Given the fact that Heads were not supposed to talk directly to applicants or potential applicants this process had a slightly surreal feel to it. Nevertheless two were actively discouraged.

> I explained [to the teacher] that there were deficiencies in one area and that I could not support her application.

Other heads indicated more subtly to teachers that their chances were slim, as their applications would not be supported:

> Not directly, but in training sessions to staff I did make criteria clear and discuss scenarios that may make it difficult to cross the threshold (e.g. recent disciplinary interview).

> The three who did not apply were all receiving support in order to improve their performance. Although no direct advice not to apply was given, they were aware of the management's view of their shortcomings.

Training alluded to standards. I gave the message not to bother if they did not meet the standards.

Other heads encouraged *all* the teaching staff to apply:

I advised all eligible to apply.

I insisted all should apply and that I would support them.

I advised all of those eligible to apply. I told them I considered them all to be worthy of success and that they should support one another by entering the fray together.

There is some evidence from our research into teachers' views and experiences, to be reported in Chapter 4, that some teachers in schools where *all* had been encouraged to apply, failed to cross the pay threshold and later discovered that their head had not supported their application in the first place. Some heads preferred to postpone making a decision and to discuss the situation with the external assessor, perhaps to get moral support for a 'standards not yet met' verdict, or even to be able to assign responsibility to the assessor.

As we found in the interviews carried out with headteachers before the process began, some of the most effective members of staff had been initially very reluctant to apply and had had to be cajoled by their head into submitting an application:

I did tell one very good teacher who is fearful of failure that he had to apply!

I persuaded two to apply who were not going to apply.

I had to encourage some to apply. They did not think they would good enough or that they would get it – often they were the *best* teachers!

Unsuccessful applicants

Since only 3 per cent of applicants were unsuccessful the numbers involved in the 28 per cent of schools where someone was turned down were bound to be small. In three-quarters of cases it was either one or two teachers. We shall be reporting more fully on unsuccessful teachers' own vantage point about their rejection in Chapter 4, but it was extremely rare for a teacher to have failed under only one of the five standards. Most teachers were judged 'not yet met' on at least two or more:

Known problems observed by me in class management; lack of colleagues' confidence in team leader; questionable pupil progress.

Poor planning; constant parental complaints; lack of support for other colleagues; negativity of attitude.

The most commonly mentioned problematic areas were Standard 2, *Teaching and Assessment*, and Standard 3, *Pupil Progress*. Within *Teaching and Assessment*, poor class management, poor teaching quality and failure to mark work were mentioned specifically.

Some heads who had judged the applications of *supply* teachers in their school pointed to the problems that this special group may face in providing evidence:

Supply teacher [was unsuccessful] who had only worked occasionally in the school and had not been formally monitored.

Two [who didn't cross the threshold] were supply teachers who had great difficulty accessing evidence. Equal opportunities issue here, since most supply teachers are female.

There were also a number of cases where heads felt unable to support teachers' applications because they believed that the evidence cited on their forms could not be substantiated and ran counter to the head's own knowledge of the teacher:

Scrutiny of planning and work samples, and lesson observations, indicated that claims made in the application were not correct.

A number of heads mentioned the *quality* of the application form itself:

Muddled application.

Woefully inadequate form. Teacher had spent 30 minutes on it.

The external threshold assessor

The role of the external threshold assessor involved going into schools to check that the procedures were being properly applied, so it was potentially extremely sensitive. A number of heads had themselves trained to be external assessors, not always with the intention of going round other schools checking their procedures, but sometimes more to be able to understand the process from the inside. Furthermore there had been a great deal of publicity about daily payments in excess of £300 and many assessors were also inspectors with the Office for Standards in Education (Ofsted). The dual role of inspector and threshold assessor could cause problems for both the school and the external appraiser, especially if the two sets of procedures employed in inspection and external assessment of performance-related pay decisions became confused.

In the event over 90 per cent of heads were satisfied with the assessors' visits and Table 3.4 shows some of the answers to questions about them. Many heads saw it as an assessment of themselves and the school, so they were pleased when all went well. They felt well informed about the structure of the visit and what was needed, though fewer than half (46 per cent) the assessors gave any indication in advance of their personal views about the applications. A few heads grumbled about the amount of documentation required and some felt the assessor was behaving too much like an Ofsted inspector, but these were a small minority of cases.

> Quite comfortable. The answer was speedy, efficient and affirmative of the work we had done.

> I am proud of what we achieved and I don't object to letting people know this or how hard my staff work and how good they are.

There was a significant minority who were irritated by the visit and found that it was time-consuming, not always relevant or in their opinion they were asked for too much. Some ventured into sarcasm to explain how they felt:

> Over the moon! It is so refreshing having another inspection by someone of doubtful ability checking up on me yet again. Clearly I cannot be trusted and I now understand that.

> More bureaucracy with inspectorial overtones.

Table 3.4 Responses of 1,239 heads to questions about the threshold assessor's visit

	Percentage
Yes, satisfied with arrangements for assessor's visit	92
Head 'well informed' or 'quite informed' about the structure of the visit	94
Assessor asked for information about school context before visit	92
Assessor discussed sample of applicants before visit	86
Assessor indicated own view of applications before visit	46
Assessor asked for teachers' evidence to be available on day of visit	90
Assessor did job 'very effectively' or 'quite effectively'	97

Providing evidence for the external assessor

Assessors had been warned in their own notes of guidance (CEA Professional Guidance Note No. 5 for Threshold Assessors dated 19 February 2001) not to be excessive in any requests for evidence. The emphasis was meant to be on verification:

> Only the focused evidence necessary to enable verification of the selected Standards of those in the sample should be requested ... Underlying all strategy in this regard must be the principle that the purpose of the threshold assessment visit is to verify and not to assess. Large volumes of evidence are neither necessary nor desirable in this regard.
>
> (CEA Professional Guidance Note No. 5)

Headteachers were asked what *type* of evidence the teachers in the sample were asked by the assessor to provide. Some simply stated that the evidence requested was tailored to support statements on individual teachers' applications. Others provided a list of different types of evidence. Most were clearly intended to provide evidence under Standards 2, *Teaching and Assessment,* and 3, *Pupil Progress*:

> Teachers' lesson plans; exam data; pupils' planners; pupils' work; schemes of work; GCSE specific material; evidence of quality teaching; assessment evidence.

> Short-term planning showing how different pupil groups have their needs met; evidence of how they mark and assess children's work: marking records, samples of books, pupil portfolios; evidence of lesson observations by SMT [senior management team] of the teacher's work.

> Whatever they [the applicants] wanted to provide. Some provided a box full – quite wore the Assessor out. It was his first job. He quickly realised he had too much evidence – here all day.

Lesson observation

This section and the following one are extremely brief, for a very good reason: there is almost nothing to report. That assessors might enter classrooms to observe lessons was a theoretical possibility, they had the option of so doing, but it was never a reality. Indeed, the teacher unions had resisted observation by external assessors very strongly, fearing that it might put them in a position to override the evidence. In practice, the emphasis was very much on paperwork, and the truth of the matter is that, out of 1,239 primary and secondary schools, only one headteacher reported that the assessor had actually observed a lesson. Hundreds of thousands of hours must have been expended nationally by assessors scrutinising paperwork and interviewing people, but virtually no time at all observing anyone teach.

Disagreements between assessors and headteachers

This section too is brief. Out of the 22,764 applicants considered by threshold assessors in the 1,239 schools in this sample, there were only 92 reported cases in 75 schools (19 primary, 56 secondary) where headteacher and assessor disagreed. This is about .4 per cent. The two parties agreed about 99.6 per cent of teachers. Inside this infinitesimal disagreement there were 58 cases where the assessor thought the teacher a failure, but not the head, and 34 cases the other way round. Some of these cases were of supply teachers, others involved long-term ill health and lack of evidence. Nearly all final decisions had been reached in an amicable manner. In only two cases was there a hint of tension in the relationship, and in both instances the internal view prevailed:

> I was able to provide enough verbal evidence and reason about why the applicant should cross the threshold and eventually convinced her.

> Each time the Assessor raised a point of contention, my team and the teacher concerned produced additional evidence to back my judgement. We refused to accept that a member of staff should fail on a technicality. Eventually he gave in.

It did not seem easy to justify the vast amount of time and effort involved and the high cost of sending threshold assessors to every school in the country, at expensive daily rates, when there was agreement over nearly 100 per cent of cases. A spot-checking verification system in some schools, or an appeals process, should one be needed, might have been more appropriate. However, teacher union officials, whose interviews are reported in Chapter 5, were keen to have external assessors in order to diminish the power and patronage of headteachers.

Overall rating of external assessors

Whether or not they are needed, assessors do appear to have been an extremely effective lubricant in what could have been a most difficult assignment. Their high approval rating from headteachers (97 per cent rated 'very effective' or 'quite effective', as shown in Table 3.4) may in part be explained by the massively high level of agreement between the two parties, but heads' written comments were also mainly positive, with few carping.

'Professional', 'efficient' and 'thorough' were descriptors of the assessors, repeated time and again by both primary and secondary headteachers. A few complaints were made about the process being too Ofsted based, or the individual assessor being an Ofsted clone, almost all from primary heads, whereas other types of comment, positive, negative or ambivalent, came equally from both sectors:

> My Threshold Assessor was excellent. She was very understanding, very hardworking and efficient.

> Must be the easiest £600 he has ever made.

> A Threshold Assessor for all schools should not be necessary. Head-teachers should be able to make this decision (if it should be made at all) with monitoring of a few schools to check consistency.

> I understand the need for the assessor to be there as a way of indicating that this is rigorous but in my experience as head and assessor, heads have carried out their role thoughtfully and professionally. I believe the assessor to be a costly addition and the bureaucracy involved in assessment is staggering.

Reactions of teachers

Heads informed most teachers (over two-thirds) individually of the outcome, though in some schools where all teachers had been successful, it was announced to the whole group. Unsuccessful teachers were almost all informed individually; only in four schools was any announcement about failure to cross the threshold made in a group context.

Successful teachers

The same words were used over and over again by headteachers to describe the reactions of their successful colleagues. Given that 97 per cent of applicants eventually received their £2,000 payment, there was much relief and celebration, and frequently a statement that success had been well deserved, since most heads saw themselves as members of the same team:

> 68 people produce different reactions. All were pleased; most believed it to be their entitlement too. There was considerable relief.

> Pleased, not surprised. Would have been incandescent had they failed!

> The whole 'team' got through – sense of shared pleasure.

> Very pleased! I got chocolates and thank you cards!

Some successful schools still experienced resentment over the elaborate processes and the considerable amount of time involved. It was a hostility to the process that heads themselves shared:

Pleased with the money. Cynical about the process.

They were very pleased and to some extent relieved. There was also a degree of resentment about being made to 'jump through hoops'.

Relief and pleasure mixed with antagonism about the whole process. Upset that they had to prove themselves and that my judgement was not sufficient.

Unsuccessful teachers

Though far fewer in number the 3 per cent of unsuccessful teachers were generally bitter. Words which featured most frequently in heads' comments were, as one might expect, 'angry', 'disappointed' and 'upset'. Some teachers were described as accepting and/or clearly determined to improve their performance. A number of heads found the experience deeply stressful and demoralising themselves, especially when their colleague was ill or was seeking redress:

Disbelief and anger immediately. Meeting finished in an unsatisfactory way and colleague became absent with stress a few days later.

Very aggressive. Is appealing. Seeking alternative employment. Bringing unions/legal advice in.

Angry and demoralised. Anger directed at headteacher.

Very bad. The teacher has almost had a nervous breakdown as a result. He was very angry. The time he spent investigating with his union and me looking at challenging the decision was a great distraction from his making progress. He was very angry and I found the whole process (threatened with grievances, resignation) very unpleasant.

Disappointed – keen to know why – what aspect of work had failed; anxious to put weaknesses right and what could they and the school do to support them?

The effect of threshold assessment on teachers and teaching

As we stated in Chapters 1 and 2, one of the major aims of performance-related pay is to improve the quality of classroom teaching by rewarding those who are thought to be doing it well. Yet questions about its impact on classroom practice are rarely addressed in research. In the eyes of headteachers in this study the impact of threshold assessment on classroom practice appears to have been minimal. Very few (2 per cent) thought it had improved classroom practice 'a lot'. Only one in five (20 per cent) thought it had had 'some' impact. Over half (53 per cent) felt it had exerted no influence at all and a further quarter (25 per cent) said it had had 'a little' effect.

There was virtually no difference when heads' assessments of the impact of threshold assessment on successful and unsuccessful applicants were analysed separately. Over three-quarters still said it had had little or no effect. The data gathered from our studies of teachers' views and experiences, reported later in this book, suggest that the main influence of threshold assessment was to persuade teachers to keep more detailed records of children's work so they would have more written evidence on a future occasion, rather than to change the way they taught.

When performance-related pay was first announced there was a fear that it might have a divisive effect in staffrooms, but that was before anyone knew how many teachers would be successful. Most heads felt the process had had little positive or negative effect on staff relations, mainly because almost all teachers had been successful. A tiny minority said that it had led to difficult staff relations, usually in their relationship with an unsuccessful candidate. In a few cases sympathy had been expressed by other staff towards the unsuccessful candidates and in one case the head had said that this had caused problems, but in the main the process was not seen as unduly influential on relationships between staff.

Heads' overall appraisal of performance-related pay (PRP)

Of the sample of 500 questionnaires analysed intensively for qualitative responses, 461 headteachers (256 secondary, 205 primary) had responded freehand to an invitation to comment on the whole issue of performance-related pay (PRP). Each headteacher's response was coded and placed under one of three main categories: Positive, Negative, and Mixed. Sub-categories were then created under each main heading. The data were also analysed separately for primary and secondary headteachers, to elicit any differences between the two.

As was explained earlier, performance-related pay can be seen in two parts: threshold assessment, which is discussed in this chapter, and performance management, the continuing process whereby teachers are encouraged and supported to improve their skill, which is discussed in later chapters. Although the question asked was *in general* about heads' attitudes to performance-related pay for teachers, it was clear that many of their comments related only to the threshold assessment part of it, so their experiences of this process may have skewed their responses. Indeed, some heads stated specifically that they felt the process had been introduced in the wrong order, in that performance management should have been the starting point, followed by threshold assessment and the rewarding of those thought to be doing well:

> It seems to have been a missed opportunity to have the first cohort judged before a year of agreed performance standards! I would have preferred standards described, then a year of performance, then threshold assessment.

Sixty per cent of headteachers indicated that they were against performance-related pay in principle. Feelings sometimes ran high on this topic:

> I am firmly opposed to it. It is a cumbersome, wasteful and degrading process.

> Totally opposed. We work in a 'difficult' area, our success comes from mutual support and high levels of collegiality. Many of the most valuable things we do for our pupils do not fit on to performance rates, including values, morals, extra-curricular experiences. Petty bonuses are divisive and attempts to prove worth are a distraction. It is a process long discredited and discarded by industry and in disrepute in National Health Service Trusts.

Only 1 per cent of respondents expressed 'mixed' feelings, while 39 per cent said they thought it was a good idea *in principle*, though many had reservations about its current practice. Several of these spoke with as much feeling in favour of the principle, as those who had railed against it:

> I think it is definitely the way forward. It motivates teachers to improve and reflect on their practice. I have never seen so much interest expressed in the Autumn Package [the school's overall performance data] … and the evaluation of school and class data!

> I am very pleased with the principle – as a headteacher I have gained from such a system – quality teachers should also gain.

However, even among those in favour of performance-related pay in principle, a large majority expressed concerns about its actual implementation. These tended to focus on their experiences with the threshold assessment procedure:

> If done properly and fairly I agree with the best teachers getting additional rewards. I believe the system devised offered an opportunity to allow this to occur. I do not believe the practice has realised the opportunity.

I am in favour in principle of PRP but I think the threshold assessment is very open ended. I think it can result in teachers being successful even if they 'fail' to carry out basic essentials of their role – e.g. their effectiveness as form teachers.

In principle I feel that good teachers should be rewarded and those who are ineffective should not. It's the volume of work collecting evidence on both groups which concerns me.

Fine in principle – however, the process is too lengthy and difficult for heads and staff. Schools need to build up a database of information to support all future applications.

Further analysis was undertaken to identify any differences in attitude between primary and secondary heads. Table 3.5 reveals that primary heads are much more opposed to PRP than their secondary counterparts, nearly three-quarters expressing negative feelings, compared with a half of secondary heads. A chi-square test showed the difference to be significant at well beyond the 0.001 level of significance (probability of occurring by chance less than one in a thousand).

One reason may be that secondary schools have for much longer had statistical data on pupil achievement and progress, and therefore this type of process is less alien to them. Another reason for this disparity lies in the sometimes different cultures of primary and secondary schools. Primary school staff see themselves more as a single team, while secondary schools, with their different subject departments and faculties, appear more fragmented. Certainly, among 'negative' primary heads, by far the largest sub-category was that relating to the potentially divisive nature of the performance pay. While just over a fifth of secondary heads expressed concern about this, the figure was a third amongst the primary heads:

I have no problem in setting targets and objectives, these are vital for development and improvement. I object to the role I had to play. I feel it drove a wedge between myself and staff – which was unnecessary and unproductive. Fortunately all applicants were successful. I dread to think of the consequences if any had been unsuccessful.

(Primary)

Table 3.5 Percentage of primary and secondary headteachers' (in 500 schools) comments about the merits of performance-related pay in principle in three categories

Phase	Positive %	Negative %	Mixed %
Primary	27	71	2
Secondary	48	50	2

Other reasons for opposition cited by both primary and secondary heads were worries about standardisation within and between schools, and philosophical and practical concerns about measuring teachers' performance, like refusing to embrace what was regarded as a factory model, with teachers as machines and pupils as output:

> I am very uncertain about relating remuneration to a crude set of performance criteria for teachers. I do not believe it practicable to reduce the job of teachers to some kind of 'productivity' measure.

> The introduction of PRP is problematic unless a fair and transparent set of criteria can be applied. We all know some teachers are more effective than others. However, how do you quantify the difference?

Those in favour did not see these issues as problematic and were enthusiastic about the opportunity to reward good teachers:

> As a former LEA officer who has observed hundreds of lessons, I feel strongly that good teachers should be rewarded.

> Jobs done well should be rewarded. Coasters should not gain additional rewards.

Perhaps the most striking feature of the comments made by 'positive' heads was the rarity of explicit references to any impact on *learning*. The focus was very much on the benefit to teachers rather than their pupils. Only two primary heads and one secondary in this supportive group referred at all to the possible repercussion for pupils:

> If managed well, it can enhance pupil performance.
>
> (Primary)

> Generally in favour of acknowledging the practice of good teachers. However, I feel the standard or pass mark should be the equivalent of Ofsted grade 3 – i.e. good teachers. This would lead to improved classroom practice.
>
> (Secondary)

Those *opposed* to the principle, a number of heads, particularly secondary, expressed the view that there would be *no* beneficial impact on either teacher performance or classroom practice but, as with responses to other questions, they were often talking within the context of this first stage of threshold assessment, rather than considering the wider picture including performance management:

Very little positive effect on teaching and learning. Negative effects – even the best teachers were concerned that they may not succeed. Gave the school an air of uncertainty, even panic, on occasions.

(Secondary)

The threshold assessment process has encouraged staff to use the school databases and staff now look far more closely at value added. However, it has not improved classroom practice and performance – teachers are not better teachers as a result of the activity.

(Primary)

For heads opposed to payment for performance the problems seemed obvious. They saw it as divisive, demotivating, impossible to implement fairly, yet another bureaucratic burden, and not likely to raise standards. The call from this group was to increase the pay of *all* teachers in order to address retention and recruitment problems, and then to deal separately with poorly performing teachers through capability procedures.

Heads in favour welcomed the *patronage* that allowed them to reward those they regarded as their good teachers, but even these enthusiasts acknowledged the problems that occur when policy is translated into practice. Moreover, they were seriously worried about the future funding implications of teachers crossing a threshold that would make them eligible to apply for further increments, and thus move even higher up the pay scale.

It also became apparent from the analysis that there were still headteachers who had not made the link between threshold assessment and performance management, the two key strands of the government's performance-related pay policy. The comment below exemplified this lack of understanding of what was going to be involved in future:

It is not 'performance-related pay'. That would involve judging teachers' performance annually and paying them on the basis of those judgements. A daunting and potentially very adversarial task.

Yet this is precisely what was intended to happen.

Some 203 headteachers decided to make additional comments, entirely of their own choosing. The majority of these were overwhelmingly negative about the process and these were primarily focused on the additional workload that this had created for both heads and teachers and that it was seen as a bureaucratic and costly exercise:

Yet another example of a badly thought through 'top of the head, I had a dream' government mentality. More paperwork for heads, more paperwork for teachers.

Crazy and expensive. I (and most heads) have shown my commitment to improving teaching and learning through undertaking, when necessary, a competence procedure, and on other occasions providing focused training and support. The teaching profession needs improved status, respect and pay (which are undeniably linked). This process has not, to my mind, assisted.

A small number of heads commented that they themselves had received no pay rise for all the work that they had incurred as a result of the process. Some expressed regret about the unfairness for those competent younger staff who had not yet reached the appropriate point on the pay scale, and so were not even eligible to apply. There was also, in a few cases, concern about the erosion of differentials between classroom teaching staff and those on leadership/deputy head scales, and about the effects on recruitment:

> Threshold assessment for all staff, not just those who are on point 9 [of the pay scale]! This has caused much discussion and heated debate and everyone believes that it should be open to all.

> Until there is a sufficient supply of good teachers, all this jumping through hoops is not helpful. If you have a Physics teacher (with a Physics degree) are you going to upset him with an 'iffy' threshold assessment? Recruitment is a far more pressing concern.

The messages from this study of 1,239 headteachers' reactions to the first stage of the government's strategy are very clear. While they did not find it difficult to assess the five standards that teachers had to meet in order to receive their £2,000 additional performance payment, they were vitriolic in their condemnation of the training they had received and the considerable amount of time they had had to spend on the exercise, on average between one and three-quarters (secondary) and two hours (primary) per teacher applicant. Furthermore the ground rules had seemed to change dramatically during their training: they were first told that relatively few teachers would be successful, then that most would go through the threshold.

Since 97 per cent of eligible teachers who applied in the first round of threshold assessment were successful, the exercise seemed more of a general pay rise than a sieving of the most competent, barely worth the time and effort involved, especially as most heads had to deal with the applications entirely on their own. This sense of futility was compounded by the usually negative reaction of the unsuccessful, some threatening action against the decision, a prospect of which heads were fearful.

Despite some initial reservations at the high rate of pay (over £300 per day at that time) earned by external assessors and the inspection background of some, most were highly respected by headteachers, well over 90 per cent feeling they had done their job skilfully and conscientiously. This may partly have been due to the extraordinarily high level of agreement between heads and assessors about the outcomes, as there was disagreement in only 0.4 per cent of cases. In later rounds, threshold assessors scrutinised applications from a sample of schools rather than in every school.

Some 60 per cent of heads were opposed to performance-related pay, but 39 per cent were in favour of it in principle, though most of these were unhappy about the way it had been put into practice. Three-quarters of heads felt threshold assessment had made little or no difference to what teachers did in the classroom. This is confirmed by our studies of teachers themselves, which suggest that they keep more careful records, rather than change how they teach. The story of teachers' own perceptions and experiences is told in Chapter 4, while headteachers' views and experiences of the performance management stage of the process will be reported in Chapter 6.

4 Success and failure

The views and experiences of teachers

The great majority of teachers in English primary and secondary schools were eligible to apply for performance-related pay in 2000, when the threshold assessment procedure was first introduced. There had been considerable recruitment of teachers two or three decades earlier, so the age distribution of the teaching population was skewed towards the more experienced, about two-thirds of teachers being over forty at the time of introduction.

This made performance-related pay a high stakes issue for teachers. Since the majority had twenty or more years of experience, they would expect, and in turn be expected, to cross any pay threshold without great difficulty. The price of failure was bound to be higher than the cash involved: loss of respect from fellow teachers, a huge blow to self-esteem, and a likely quarrel with anyone involved in the decision. There was considerable tension, therefore, when plans were announced, especially as early messages had suggested that relatively few might be successful. Even when it was known that most were expected to progress to the higher salary scale (upper pay spine), there was still unease until the position of individuals was confirmed. Some teachers went so far as to say they would not even demean themselves to apply, since they were against performance-related pay in principle.

In this chapter we examine the experiences of three groups of teachers, a total of 398 respondents in all. Each group completed an initial questionnaire, and a sizeable sub-sample (233) responded to a follow-up questionnaire. Some were also interviewed. The three group sample was made up as below, the two figures against each showing the numbers who responded to the initial and follow-up questionnaire respectively:

1 Teachers who applied to cross the threshold and were successful (117 + 72)
2 Teachers who applied and were unsuccessful (180 + 111)
3 Teachers who were eligible to apply, but chose not to (101 + 50).

Surveys of these groups were undertaken using questionnaires containing both closed and open questions. All the teachers taking part were volunteers, so unlike the stratified random sample of headteachers reported in Chapter 3, these were *opportunity samples*. In the event 97 per cent of teachers were successful nationally, so the first of the three groups is drawn from a massive constituency, the other two from relatively small ones.

Teachers who applied and were successful

Headteachers of 31 primary and secondary schools who had themselves taken part in the case study element of our research agreed to distribute letters to their staff asking for teachers who might be willing to participate in the research. We did not, at this first stage, distinguish between those eligible to apply to cross the threshold in 2000 and those ineligible, as we were interested to investigate the views of *all* teachers of what were new procedures. A total of 178 teachers responded to this letter. In-depth interviews were carried out with 20 teachers in three different regions, and questionnaires were sent to the remainder. Completed questionnaires were received from 117 teachers, of whom 93 (80 per cent) were eligible to apply to cross the threshold and only five had decided not to apply.

Once teachers had been notified of the outcome of their application to cross the threshold, a second questionnaire was sent to the 83 teachers who had completed the initial questionnaire and said they were prepared to complete a follow-up questionnaire. Completed questionnaires were returned by 72 teachers. All of these had been successful in crossing the threshold, though we could not have predicted this at the time of the original questionnaire.

Teachers' views on performance-related pay

In the summer of 2000, before teachers knew the outcome of their application to cross the threshold, we asked the 117 teachers completing the first questionnaire their views on performance-related pay (PRP). The first item offered them statements grounded in data gathered previously in interviews with heads and teachers, inviting agreement or disagreement on a forced choice four-point scale, with no central 'don't know' or 'neutral' point (see Table 4.1).

The key concern emerging from teachers' mainly negative responses to these statements was their *concept of professionalism*, which seemed to be based on two major precepts: (1) that teachers should work as a team; (2) that they should be intrinsically motivated. A very large majority (80 per cent) believed that it would threaten staff relationships, be *divisive*, even more (87 per cent) fearing that favouritism could influence who receives additional payments. If the government's intention was to raise teaching standards, the message was not encouraging, since 67 per cent of teachers did not feel it would raise standards of teaching, while 71 per cent felt it would have no impact on levels of pupil attainment. About a quarter of the

Table 4.1 Views of 117 teachers on the principles of performance-related pay before decisions were known

	Strongly agree %	Agree %	Disagree %	Strongly disagree %
It will encourage good teachers to stay in the classroom	7	30	46	18
It will cause bad feeling amongst staff	36	44	17	4
It will reward hard-working teachers	13	38	37	11
There is a danger of favouritism	24	63	11	2
It will encourage teachers to work harder	3	23	53	22
Teachers will ignore important elements of their work that are not measurable	21	42	32	5
It will encourage poor teachers to leave the profession	3	24	64	9
It will raise teaching standards	1	33	52	15
It will help to improve standards of pupils' attainment	0	28	55	16
It will present a positive picture of the profession to parents and the general public	5	25	55	15

Note: Percentages do not always add up to 100 because of rounding.

teachers surveyed believed that performance-related pay would 'encourage poor teachers to leave the profession' and, as will be discussed later in this chapter, there was evidence that some teachers who were unsuccessful in their bid to cross the threshold did indeed quit teaching.

The second question sought to elicit views about any likely impact on teachers' practice: 'Do you think that the linking of increments to annual performance reviews will have any impact on your future practice?' This invoked the notion of intrinsic motivation, as 62 per cent said 'No', while 38 per cent replied 'Yes'. Half of those who indicated there would be *no* impact stated that they were already working as hard as they could:

> I'm working flat out as it is. I don't think I can honestly take on any more work or give much more.

> I always give my all for the sake of the pupils.

> I have always tried to improve my performance, without financial incentive, as a matter of professional pride.

> I don't need extrinsic motivation – it is the wrong job to be in for monetary gain!

Training/guidance on threshold assessment

Headteachers had received training for their role in the threshold process, even though it was not thought to have been very good. Teachers did not have any official training, though they received documentation and could access the Department for Education and Employment website. Their training and advice came from a variety of other sources, including in-service training days, and they also regarded the advice they received from their unions as important and valuable. The views and experiences of teacher union officials are described in the next chapter.

Preparation for the threshold assessment process had been undertaken in most schools. This had focused on the structure and timescale for completing the process and, in some schools, on how to complete the application form. Such sessions were often led by the head, but in secondary schools it was common for other senior managers to be involved. Of the 93 eligible teachers in our questionnaire survey, 80 per cent had received threshold *documentation* from their teacher union with a further 8 per cent saying they had been given *verbal* advice by their local representative. However they had gathered the information, 82 per cent of teachers said they felt 'quite' or 'well' informed about the process before completing the application form.

Teachers' views of the threshold 'standards'

In order to elicit teachers' views of the standards they had to meet in order to cross the threshold, the questionnaire included a set of statements made previously by heads and teachers in interviews and asked the teachers to indicate the extent to which they agreed or disagreed with these statements. Table 4.2 shows some of the key findings.

Table 4.2 Teachers' views on the threshold 'standards' ($n = 117$)

	Strongly agree %	Agree %	Disagree %	Strongly disagree %
They are the sort of things that most teachers are doing already	41	55	3	1
They will be difficult for teachers to achieve	1	11	75	13
Expecting teachers to achieve in all five areas discriminates against some good teachers	22	35	38	5
They help teachers reflect on their practice	14	66	13	7
They will encourage teachers to ignore important elements of their work which are not measurable	22	44	29	5
Heads will not be able to assess if teachers are reaching the standards	11	33	48	8

Teachers had virtually no quarrel with the actual content of the required standards, the overwhelming majority (96 per cent) believing they encompassed roles, responsibilities, knowledge and skills which good teachers should undertake and display every day of their professional career. Yet over half believed that even good teachers might not meet all the standards, while two-thirds agreed that teachers might start to give priority to those areas of work for which they were accountable, and neglect those not within the process. A large minority (44 per cent) also questioned whether headteachers had the information available to assess whether teachers had met the standards required. Classroom observation by heads was relatively rare at that time, especially in secondary schools, where it was often the head of department who undertook monitoring. A wide range of practice emerged, ranging from three or more observations a year to none at all. Some 38 per cent of secondary teachers in the sample indicated that their line manager had *never once* observed their teaching. The introduction of threshold assessment had brought about certain changes to the monitoring of teachers' performance, 17 per cent of teachers indicating additions to existing systems, the majority of these being the inclusion of, or an increase in classroom observations.

Pupil progress

Teachers encountered a number of problems providing evidence to prove they had met the required standards under each of the five main headings. The standard causing the least difficulty was *Knowledge and Understanding*, with nearly three-quarters indicating that they had found this 'quite' or 'very' easy. Two-thirds also reported few problems with *Teaching and Assessment*, *Wider Professional Effectiveness* and *Professional Characteristics*.

It was the *Pupil Progress* standard which presented the greatest difficulty for teachers, nearly two-thirds stating that it had been 'quite' or 'very' difficult to provide supporting evidence for it. The stated requirement for achieving this standard was:

> ... as a result of your teaching, your pupils achieve well relative to their prior attainment, making progress as good or better than similar pupils nationally. This should be shown in marks or grades in any relevant national tests or examinations, or school-based assessment for pupils where national tests and examinations are not taken.
>
> (DfEE 2000c: 4)

Primary teachers found it more problematic to produce statistical data on pupil progress than their secondary counterparts, but there was also a variety of response to this question amongst secondary teachers. Several said their school had had in place for some years comprehensive pupil progress monitoring systems, whereby 'value added' scores were regularly calculated, while other schools had only recently started to use such performance data.

Several teachers claimed not to understand the figures obtained, suggesting a need for in-service training in this area, if statistics are to be of use to classroom practitioners:

> I would have liked a clearer explanation of how to interpret statistics [and Cognitive Abilities Test] scores ... We were given lots of data but most of it made little sense to me.

The whole area of using pupil progress measurement to identify the most effective teachers, or pay people more, is a contentious one. A number of problems have been identified (Goldstein 2001). They include the following:

- most performance data are for a longer period than a single year
- different models used to calculate 'value added' will result in different outcomes
- pupil mobility raises problems for all analyses of performance
- no one teacher should be held singly responsible for the progress or otherwise of children in his/her class.

In secondary schools, pupils' experiences in other subject areas with other teachers, as well as their general attitude towards school, may be more important than the impact of one teacher. What is happening outside school can dramatically affect rates of progress.

The external threshold assessor

In the first round of the threshold assessment, an external *threshold assessor* was assigned to every school in which a teacher or teachers had applied, though this requirement was subsequently dropped in later cycles. Their role was to scrutinise a sample of the applications, already judged by the headteacher as meeting or not meeting the standards, in order to ensure the procedure had been properly implemented. The size of the sample was related to the number of teachers applying in any school, with a maximum of ten. The assessor could ask teachers within the sample to provide documentary evidence to support their application.

The role of the external threshold assessor had been a contentious one. Generally, the teacher unions were in favour of an external reviewer to ensure that heads were acting in accordance with the agreed procedures and in a fair manner, but the teachers in our study were divided in their opinions. While the majority were in favour of an impartial assessor to verify that the head had carried out the process properly, a large minority believed that their headteacher should be trusted, and some felt strongly that an external assessor could not judge their teaching merely by reading an application form. Cambridge Education Associates (CEA), the private company responsible for the deployment and management of assessors, made it very clear that the assessor's principal role was to ensure heads had followed the procedures, not to assess individual applications. If headteachers were able to provide evidence of systematic monitoring and evaluation of teaching taking place in the school, then it was unlikely that their judgement about individual teachers would be challenged.

Communications between head and teacher

The way in which the threshold assessment process was handled provides a rich insight into some headteachers' managerial skills, or lack of them. As was reported in Chapter 3 many heads found the whole process quite stressful, so considerable secrecy often surrounded the processing of applications, leaving many teachers ignorant of what was happening. Among the successful, 20 per cent did not know, even after they had been told the outcome, whether their headteacher had *initially* supported their application. When asked who, the head or the external assessor, had made the *final* decision about the outcome of their application, about half indicated that they did not know.

The majority of the successful teachers were informed of their achievement by their headteacher, though in a small number of secondary schools this task had been delegated to their line manager. The way in which the information had initially been imparted varied considerably. In schools where everyone had been successful, the head often announced it in whole staff meetings or placed a notice on the staffroom board. Some said they had been told during the course of an *informal* conversation with the head, while others had received a letter or a phone call at home, but only a small number indicated that they had been told of their success in a *formal* meeting with the head.

It was a requirement of the threshold procedure that application forms should be returned to teachers after the external assessor's visit, when the outcome was known, but 85 per cent said they had *not* received their application form with the head's comments. Most were not concerned about this. Where feedback was given, it was often perfunctory, though some clearly valued this acknowledgement of their work:

> Were I to wish to leave the school or apply for an internal promotion, it would help me to formulate a better application. I had not realised that my headteacher thought so highly of me.

Effect on morale

During intensive interviews with 20 teachers in the early stages of the research, it had become clear that the work involved in completing the application form and assembling evidence, placed further unwanted pressure on teachers. This was also reflected in the questionnaires, 65 per cent of teachers stating that the introduction of the threshold assessment process had made a 'quite' or 'very' negative impact on staff morale. Only 10 per cent referred to any positive impact.

Success soon changed this position. Responses to the question about staff morale in the follow-up questionnaire showed that the success of their applications, and the receipt of the £2,000 additional payment, had brought about a transformation in some teachers' feelings about the whole threshold assessment procedure. At the beginning of the process not a single teacher had felt that threshold assessment was having a 'very positive' effect on staff morale, while over two-thirds (68 per cent) had said its impact was 'quite' or 'very negative'. A year later over a quarter (28 per cent) felt its impact had been 'quite' or 'very positive' and only 38 per cent, still a significant minority, described it as having exerted a 'quite' or 'very negative' effect.

Teachers who applied but were unsuccessful

The high stakes nature of an appraisal and reward system for an ageing profession was pointed out above. Once it was known that 97 per cent of teachers applying to cross the threshold in the first round of this procedure had been successful, the position of the minority who were *unsuccessful*, often a single teacher in a primary school, or perhaps two in a secondary school, became extremely difficult. The somewhat coy official expression for failure to reach the required standards was the term 'not yet met', suggesting that the decision was not necessarily a final one.

There were several differences between schools in the way the procedure was approached and undertaken. Some teachers experienced relationship problems with heads; the support available to them varied. The procedure caused particular problems for 'non-standard' teachers, such as advisory or learning support staff, supply teachers, part-timers, and those who taught children outside a school.

Contact was made with 'unsuccessful' teachers during June 2001 in two ways: via teacher unions and by a letter from the Project Director to the *Times Educational Supplement* asking for volunteers. The research team produced a flyer giving information about the Teachers' Incentive Pay Project, with a form for teachers interested in participating in the research to complete and return, using a freepost address. A questionnaire was sent to teachers who volunteered to take part. Anonymity was guaranteed to all those participating in the research.

Requests for questionnaires were received from 244 teachers and 174 were returned completed. In addition, six advisory/learning support staff took part in the research: two were interviewed, and four completed a questionnaire modified to take account of their particular circumstances, making an overall total of 180 in this sample. These six are discussed below in the section 'Teachers in non-standard settings'. Some teachers not returning the questionnaire telephoned to say that, although they had wanted to participate, they had found revisiting the events to complete the questionnaire too stressful.

The first questionnaire contained a mix of open and closed questions. It sought personal details about the teacher including sex, years in teaching, type of school, nature of employment, year group/subjects taught, years in school where the application to cross the threshold was submitted, and whether the teacher held a responsibility post. Respondents were asked whether their head had supported their application, whether they had met with the threshold assessor, what sort of evidence had been requested, who had made the final decision that their application should be unsuccessful, how they were notified of the outcome and by whom, whether they had received any feedback, the type of advice if any given to them by their union, whether they intended to seek a review of the judgement, and the effect on their classroom performance and morale.

As the questionnaires were anonymous it was not possible to triangulate the data by investigating the views of some of the other individuals involved in these cases, such as the headteacher. Of the 174 teachers who completed the first questionnaire, about three-quarters (74 per cent) decided to seek a review of the outcome, so they were sent a follow-up questionnaire by the research team. The fraction of teachers nationally asking for the decision to be reviewed was approximately a quarter, so this sample may be representative of those unsuccessful teachers who were particularly proactive, or whose feelings were especially strong. Of the 174 teachers, 85 per cent indicated they were employed on a full-time basis, 53 per cent held a responsibility post at the time of their threshold application and a number of respondents were heads of department. Fifty-six per cent worked in secondary schools, 42 per cent in primary schools and 2 per cent in special schools. Six of the teachers in the sample were supply teachers. Sixty-one per cent of the sample were female, reflecting the gender imbalance in the profession.

Threshold assessors' visits

Unsuccessful teachers were highly likely to have been included in the sample of cases looked at in detail by the external assessor (87 per cent). Some believed their inclusion in the sample meant they were more likely to fail because their application was being scrutinised, whilst those of other colleagues were not. In fact, external assessors were required to scrutinise a sample *representative* of all applications in a school. Since 97 per cent of teachers nationally were successful, and most schools had no failures at all, it became highly likely, therefore, that a school's one, or possibly two failures would be included in this representative sample.

Out of 151 unsuccessful teachers who had been included in their school's sample, 131 reported that they had been asked to make available for the external assessor's visit evidence to support their application. In some cases, little detail had been given to the teacher of the evidence required. In general, however, comprehensive lists of evidence had apparently been issued by the threshold assessor via the headteacher. One secondary teacher described such a list which contained many different items:

... schemes of work, topic plans, lesson plans, pupils' books, evidence of use of various strategies used and behaviour management, use of differentiation, departmental assessment scheme, records for pupils at entry/general level, criteria/topic specific records, progress records and progress reports to parents, monitoring and evaluation informing planning, formal test results for topics, full records of Year 9 Standard Assessment Tasks, certificate of external accreditation, notes for in-service training sessions.

The qualitative data were scrutinised to see if there were any differences between the demands made on primary teachers and their secondary peers, but none were found. The type and amount of evidence requested appeared to relate more to individual external assessors than the phase of schooling. Assessors interviewed by the research team claimed that heads sometimes asked their staff for additional documentation not requested by them.

Responses from teachers to the requests for evidence varied. Some had felt quite relaxed about the process, with no suspicion that they would be unsuccessful:

I thought the assessor would want to see 'Planning and Assessment' [one of the standards], so I was well prepared.

I expected to pass easily, so I thought it was just a formality. I handed in thirteen folders of evidence but was told this needed to be simplified so I handed in something more manageable.

Irritation was caused when demands were vaguely defined, or where large amounts of evidence were requested and a limited amount of time was available in which to supply the required documents. Some were angry that the assessor was not obliged to watch them teach:

How I wish [the assessor] had [observed]!

I wish he had, as I have had excellent classroom observations in both subjects.

Communications between head and teacher

Many heads found it difficult to discuss potential failure with teachers. Over two-thirds of the unsuccessful teachers reported that their headteacher had given no indication of whether an application from them to cross the threshold would be received favourably:

[The head] indicated that everyone on the staff eligible to apply should and stated he guaranteed everyone who applied in the first round would get [through the] threshold (over 50 staff).

She said she would fully support my application.

The deputy head helped me to complete the proforma and checked it, leading me to believe it was acceptable.

Many of these teachers did not find out until their application form was returned to them, nearly a year later, that their head had not originally supported them in their bid to cross the threshold, and there was often uncertainty about who had made the *final* decision on their application.

It was not easy to tell teachers that their competence had been questioned, but only two teachers in the sample of school-based unsuccessful teachers were not informed of the decision directly by the headteacher. Table 4.3 shows that teachers were given the news in a variety of ways, though over a third were not told face to face, receiving a letter or a telephone call.

The figures in Table 4.3 reveal contrasting approaches of headteachers in dealing with this issue. The qualitative data indicate even more starkly how some heads tried to communicate in a professional manner, while others were less meticulous:

I was invited to meet the Head who then outlined the situation. The meeting was formal although friendly.

In my classroom at the end of the day in a sealed envelope with no verbal communication at all.

Mobile phone during lunch hour.

I was informed by the Head in a corridor full of pupils. All the seven unsuccessful applicants were informed in a similar way: corridors, classrooms and school yard etc.

At our school, I and colleagues only found out whether our applications had been successful by comparing pay slips in January! There was no previous notification.

Table 4.3 How were you *first* notified that your application had been unsuccessful?

Method of notification of outcome	Percentage
Individually – formal meeting with head	36
Individually – by letter	27
Individually – told informally by head	25
Individually – by telephone	9
Not told – realised when received payslip*	2
As a group – informally	1

Note: * These teachers came from the same school.

Only 15 per cent of the *successful* teachers studied in the present project said that their head had returned their application form to them at the end of the process so they could see the heads' comments, but headteachers had been more conscientious about returning *unsuccessful* teachers' application forms, where the figure was 88 per cent. However, this difference is largely due to the fact that, in order to appeal against the original judgement, teachers had to retrieve their original application to include with their review application, so they were more likely to press their headteacher for its return.

The nature of the feedback was, in general, little more than an expansion of the list of areas in which the teacher had 'not yet met' the standard. Most heads made no attempt to use the procedure as a basis for bringing about future improvements. Many of the unsuccessful teachers reported that they had received no helpful insights into how to change or develop their practice in order to meet the standards in future. Once teachers discovered that 97 per cent of their fellows had been successful nationally, they became very disgruntled at being given no support or advice on how to improve their performance.

The 135 unsuccessful teachers who *had* received feedback were asked how they had felt about the reasons given for the rejection of their application. Only seven teachers said they felt the decision was 'probably justified'. Two further teachers, one supply and one part-timer, said they had not expected to pass because, in their particular situation, it was very difficult to prove pupil progress. The case of these special groups is discussed later in this chapter.

The most common words used in responses were 'shocked', 'furious', 'demoralised', or a combination of all three. The decisions were regarded as subjective and based on a personal bias against them; the reasons given considered to be inadequate, unfounded, unfair, and untrue. The comments below give a flavour of how these teachers reacted:

Sickened, deskilled, demotivated, loyalty to school gone, commitment gone. Had no idea that I was considered a failure – 'the weakest link' was quoted – really good for my self-esteem!

Completely destroyed. The head never saw me teach. I was never informed of any concerns about my teaching. My teaching was never monitored. Nothing was ever offered to me to support any problems it suddenly appears I have.

Furious. Both 'reasons' are totally untrue. Colleagues are equally angry and know as well as I do that I was targeted because I am the union rep. They have sent statements of support to include in my review application.

There was extreme dissatisfaction with what they saw as the 'subjective', 'biased', 'malicious' and 'vindictive' nature of the assessment. Many teachers who had been in previous disputes with their heads believed that their applications had not been objectively judged and that they were victims of management bullying. There were claims that union representatives were over-represented nationally amongst the unsuccessful teachers, a matter which will be covered in more detail in Chapter 5. The NUT also identified older teachers as less likely to have been successful, possibly because of an ideological objection to the process or because they had not been able to keep up to date and 'maintain their critical edge'. It is not possible to say whether these allegations had substance because of the relative smallness of the sample.

It is difficult to overstate the humiliation felt by unsuccessful teachers, particularly when they were the only one in their school who had been unsuccessful:

> It was a terribly humiliating experience and leaves me feeling helpless about even improving my teaching, and wary of performance management.

> It is hard going into my school where everybody passed. It makes me feel as though I am not as good as them. It is also a stigma because it was advertised as a pay rise for most teachers – I am now one of the 'few'.

The review procedure

When the requirements for the threshold assessment procedure were originally laid down, no right to appeal was included. This was inserted later following a successful high court action by the National Union of Teachers. A new job had to be created, therefore, that of the Review Assessor, whose official role was as follows:

1 to make sure that the review form has been completed correctly and that it has been received within the appropriate timescale
2 to look at the grounds on which the review has been submitted and to call for evidence
3 to consider all the evidence and make a decision
4 to log the procedure as it has happened
5 to lodge all paperwork with CEA where procedures are checked.

There was no formal contact between the Review Assessor and the original threshold assessor unless there was a need to seek confirmation of, for example, an illegible comment in the records. Review Assessors were not allowed to ask for *new* evidence, only evidence which should have been available originally. Observation of teaching was again not included in the process.

Over three-quarters of the original sample of 174 unsuccessful teachers decided to seek a review. Those who had decided not to appeal cited various reasons, including the desire to avoid further anxiety and concerns about the long-term impact on their career of openly confronting their headteacher:

> I have been unable to work for the past month as it has been the final humiliation. I have suffered at the hands of the head in front of a very young staff. There is only so much one can take.

> I am not seeking a Review because it is my opinion against the head's and he is very unlikely to acknowledge that he could misinterpret evidence.

> With so much secrecy and the almost complete disregard for the rules which the head seems to have displayed in all this, I am reluctant to take any steps which might produce short-term advantage but be to my disadvantage in the longer term.

A second questionnaire was distributed to the 134 teachers, of whom 111 completed it. Information was sought on: the length of time the review procedure had taken, any help or advice they had received in the compilation of their review application, the grounds on which they had sought their review, whether their headteacher had supported it, whether they had had any contact with the Review Assessor, and the outcome of their review. Unsuccessful appellants were asked if they intended to reapply the following year. Three-quarters of those who appealed had waited between 3–5 months to hear, while 16 per cent had waited for six months or more, a period far exceeding the 70 days originally promised as the timescale.

Completing the review application

The 111 teachers who completed the second questionnaire were asked if they had received any help in completing their review application form and, if so, from whom. As Table 4.4, indicates, the main sources of information at this time were the teacher unions, either at local or national level.

Interviews undertaken with officials from the teacher unions showed that unsuccessful teachers who went to their unions could receive different advice. The NUT advised its members to apply for a review, but the NASUWT officer had told its casework officers to treat the issue as they would any other problem and examine all the evidence before giving advice. Over three-quarters of the teachers reported that they had found the review application form 'quite' or 'very' difficult to complete:

> If I had not had union help and advice on the way in which the review could be worded and on the aspects of my application I could focus on, I would have found it extremely difficult to fill in. There was no real indication of what was required or how to set it out.

Table 4.4 Sources of help used by teachers completing review application forms (*n* = 111)

Sources of help	Percentage
Local teacher union representative	51
National teacher union helpdesk	30
Head teacher	6
Senior manager/line manager	6
Colleague in same school	19
Colleague in another school	8
Other (usually partner)	14
No help received	17

Note: These figures do not total 100 per cent as some teachers ticked more than one box.

> Very stressful to keep reliving the 'failure'.

> Time consuming, finding yet more evidence, photocopying previous evidence shown to the threshold assessor. Emotionally very difficult as I had to counteract the head's negative attitude, half truths and downright lies.

Grounds for review

Teachers were required to indicate on the Review Application form their reasons for seeking a review under three headings:

> I would have met the threshold standards if the head or assessor who made the assessment:
>
> 1 Had taken proper account of relevant evidence ☐
>
> 2 Had not taken account of irrelevant or inaccurate evidence ☐
>
> 3 Had not been biased or had not discriminated against me ☐
>
> (from the CEA Review Application Form)

As Table 4.5 shows, the data indicate that a large minority of teachers cited all three. Option 1 was cited by 91 per cent of respondents, option 2 by 63 per cent and option 3 by 69 per cent.

In only 15 per cent of the cases did the headteacher support the teacher's appeal, not surprising, given that the head had usually been the instigator of the original 'unsuccessful' verdict. Where the head did support the appeal it was often either a new head at the original school, or the headteacher of the school to which the teacher had since moved.

Table 4.5 Teachers' grounds for seeking a review (*n* = 111)

Grounds for seeking a review	Percentage
Ground 1 only	18
Ground 2 only	1
Ground 3 only	3
Grounds 1 and 2	13
Grounds 1 and 3	17
Grounds 2 and 3	6
All grounds	43

Note: These figures do not total 100 due to rounding.

About a quarter of teachers who appealed actually spoke to their Review Assessor, sometimes on the telephone. Meetings ranged from 15 minutes to two hours. An officer of Cambridge Education Associates (CEA) stressed, in interview, that if Review Assessors made a 'site visit' to a school, they were required to interview both the head and the teacher:

> What they cannot ask for is *new* evidence. What they can ask for is *further* evidence. They can only ask for evidence that should have been available to the original assessor ... Any evidence requested from the head or evidence requested from the teacher is copied to the headteacher and they know it's copied and vice-versa. So the evidence requested is very, very transparent. The whole process is.

Outcomes

Teachers were notified of the outcome of their review by letter from Cambridge Education Associates. Of the 111 teachers completing the second questionnaire, over a third (36 per cent) were successful at review. Further analysis showed there was no correlation between the grounds cited and the outcome of the review. However, teachers whose headteachers, whether new ones or the head who had judged the original application, had supported their review application were more likely to be successful. A chi-square test showed this difference to be significant at the 0.02 level, i.e. such a result would only have occurred by chance on one occasion in fifty.

A mixture of emotions was expressed by teachers who had been successful in contesting their failure:

> [I feel] justified that I knew I was right all along. But now I feel the need for action to be taken against the unprofessional conduct of the head-teacher – who can carry on and do the same thing to someone else!

> Relieved. I now have parity with my colleagues, but I'm cross that I was put through it!

Satisfied. But very angry at all the extra work I have had to do just before our school's Ofsted inspection. Very angry at my head (who has fortunately left).

Those teachers who had been unsuccessful were cynical about the review procedure:

The original assessor overturned 5 of the 8 judgements made against me by the head. For the Review Assessor to overturn the other three would be to say that their own person [the original threshold assessor] and the head were wrong. This would be 'politically' disadvantageous.

I think it is very difficult for the Review Assessor to overturn the original assessor and the headteacher. I was very disappointed that neither the original assessor nor the Review Assessor met me or ever saw me teach.

For these teachers, the desolation, demoralisation and disillusionment which they had felt when learning of their original failure to cross the threshold returned in full measure.

Of the 70 teachers who were still unsuccessful (two teachers did not report the outcome), even after the review, half said they were intending to reapply in Round 2 of the process. Nine teachers had already left teaching, either through resignation or early retirement. Six said they were unable to face possible further humiliation, while four judged further applications 'pointless', as they were still working with the same head.

Most of the 35 teachers reapplying in Round 2 were optimistic about the outcome of their second application. Over half the teachers had by then moved school, or had a new headteacher who had said they would support them; the remainder had been assured by their head (the original one) that their application would be supported, though one teacher commented wryly:

Apparently I have improved dramatically this year so the head feels that he can support me. In fact, he even offered help this time and went over my application before I finally submitted it – no alterations were necessary.

Teachers in non-standard settings

For some teachers working in 'non-standard' situations (such as advisory teachers and learning support staff, supply teachers, home tutors and part-timers), the frustrations of the application form, providing and accessing evidence and awaiting outcomes, were exacerbated by the inappropriateness of the procedure to their particular posts. The process appeared to have been designed without consideration for such groups. Union officers commented in interview:

There are those who were on short-term contracts or supply in a number of places. We have a considerable membership of people who are not school-based – LEA functionaries, Special Educational Needs or Advisory teachers. Many of them are just left floundering and the application form is so secondary-school subject based. Where does the peripatetic advisory teacher fit in?

(Union officer of the Professional Association of Teachers, PAT)

The centrally attached, like advisory teachers, contacted us to ask 'Who's doing my threshold?' There have been disproportionately more of those than classroom teachers ... We put out advice specific to primary, secondary and special; to teachers in non-standard settings and some guidance for headteachers as well.

(Union officer of NASUWT)

We did a special set of advice for centrally-employed teachers and non-attached teachers. It was really difficult for them. I think they were the ones that the DfEE didn't think about when they designed that form and that process. I honestly think they forgot about them.

(Union officer of NUT)

Training was limited to about half a dozen events around the country and we targeted it at people who would otherwise have got no access to any kind of training, peripatetic teachers, or those where they thought the head really didn't have a clue!

(Union officer of ATL)

Six 'non-standard' teachers who had been unsuccessful took part in this research. Such staff were subject to Direct Assessment, whereby a team of threshold assessors visited over a number of days to carry out the assessment. Non-standard teachers were amongst the last personnel to learn the outcome of their application, over a year after they had submitted it.

Unlike primary and secondary teachers based in schools, the advisory/learning support staff had no idea, when they submitted their application, who would assess it. They had only been told that it would not be their direct line manager. From the outset, they found the application form inappropriate. It was hard for them to provide evidence to support their case:

It's difficult to identify and supply *evidence* [to show] that [my] advice/input has had a direct effect upon pupil progress. Generally, progress relies upon Special Needs Co-ordinators etc. taking/following advice.

I was not prepared to make a nuisance of myself digging up Individual Education Plans etc. from schools I have worked at over the past three years, or alternatively inventing material.

Some felt extremely let down by the whole process. One teacher told how she was one of six staff in her support service who all failed to cross the threshold.

Many of the problems faced by advisory/learning support staff were also faced by supply teachers, whose problem was that they were assessed in the same way as teachers who only work in one school. These had to choose a headteacher, from one of the many schools they had worked in, to act as their line manager for threshold assessment purposes. Even teachers who were well known in a school immediately encountered problems:

> As a supply teacher at one school for fourteen years on a regular basis, I asked the headteacher to be my line manager. She pointed out that she would not be able to say I had met with criteria regarding evidence, but was willing to take on that role.

The criterion *Pupil Progress* was cited in all the unsuccessful supply teachers' cases. As a consequence supply teachers were extremely bitter about the threshold assessment procedure. The teacher below summed up how this group felt:

> I am an *ace* and a professional supply teacher and am regarded as such by my many colleagues in a variety of schools over a wide area. How can my qualities as a teacher be measured with statistics that do not enter into the scheme of my work? ... The only fair way to assess a supply teacher is to follow her round for a week as she goes to a different school and age-group every day (including nursery and special needs) taking assemblies, whole school singing, two classes together to release a teacher etc. You really do have to be ready for anything and with great enthusiasm ... The most practical and fair ideal would be to ask their headteachers 'Is [s/he] a talented teacher and an asset to your school?'

Of the 174 unsuccessful teachers in the main sample, 20 were employed on a part-time basis. Unlike the advisory teachers, learning support staff and supply teachers, the majority of these teachers did not suggest that the threshold assessment procedure was inappropriate to the part-time nature of their employment, and their responses to questions were more similar to those of full-time unsuccessful teachers. In secondary schools part-time subject teachers often taught particular groups throughout a school year, so collecting pupil progress data was not especially problematic. One part-timer was told she had not attended enough courses. She felt particularly bitter, because she had only worked one day a week in the period relevant to her application.

Two of the part-timers were primary teachers who shared a post. In both cases their job share partner had crossed the threshold while they had not, and 'lack of pupil progress' was cited. Both teachers found this reason difficult to accept. As one of them put it:

My morale is rock bottom. I am a part-time job share teacher and my other half job share got across the threshold and I didn't. I was told my pupils had not made progress, so I feel confused that, for the days I taught, the children made *no* progress, and the days my other half worked, they did!

Clearly, there is an issue here for school managers. What is reasonable to expect from their part-time staff? Should they be expected to attend the same number of training sessions as their full-time colleagues and events such as meetings held on days when they are not normally in school, and should they be expected to be involved in extra-curricular activities?

Eligible teachers who chose not to apply

When performance-related pay was introduced some teachers said they would not apply on principle. In order to explore eligible teachers' motives for not applying at all, the Project Director placed an appeal in the *Times Educational Supplement* for teachers who had deliberately chosen not to apply for threshold assessment to contact the research team. As a result 146 questionnaires were distributed and of these 101 were returned completed. The sample consisted mainly of full-time teachers who also held a responsibility post. Three-quarters were female and a quarter male, reflecting once more the gender imbalance within the teaching profession. Just over half were employed in secondary schools, the remainder of the sample was made up of teachers employed in primary schools and a small number who worked in special schools.

Many respondents stated that they saw the whole process as 'divisive' and therefore the majority viewed it negatively. It was also seen as an added burden:

In principle I was against it as I consider the school a community where everyone, at best, supports everyone else … I considered that it could be divisive as anti community 'esprit'. When we, as teachers, have an effective appraisal system, Ofsted, is it really necessary?

I considered it to be a divisive initiative that would contribute to the breaking down of a unified pay structure. I also thought that it was another example of the obsession with statistics – an obsession that consistently fails to give due recognition to teachers working in exceptionally difficult circumstances.

Most respondents, like the one below, felt that their headteacher would have supported their application if they had applied:

The headteacher was keen for all members of staff to apply … she expressed disappointment but respected my decision.

The main stated reason for not applying was one of *principle*: they simply objected to the very concept of performance-related pay and did not like having to 'prove their worth'. Some also cited dislike of the bureaucracy involved, lack of evidence and time, and a quarter feared that they might not be successful, though the majority felt that they would have been. It was the *Pupil Progress* standard that most believed would have caused them the greatest difficulty.

Once these teachers became aware that the vast majority of those who applied, some 97 per cent, had in fact been successful in crossing the threshold, a large number changed their attitude. About 60 per cent felt that they would now apply in a future round, many commenting that they too deserved a pay rise. More poignantly a number mentioned their fear that failure to progress through the pay threshold might in future be seen as a stigma, rather than a principled objection, and could even affect their employment prospects one day. Most of those who did eventually decide to apply believed they would be supported by their head and would be successful in crossing the threshold:

> I would be cutting off my nose to spite my face. Everyone – no matter how inept – gets it anyway (!!) so it's rather galling to be paid less than someone who is clearly less competent than myself.

> Financial considerations and no-one is fighting it any more.

There were, however, those who were adamant they would still not apply in Round 2 and they gave similar reasons for not applying as they had done in Round 1:

> My position in principle to this divisive measure. My unwillingness to spend yet more 'free' time completing huge forms.

> The principles upon which I based my first decision have not changed. Financially I will be obliged to jump through this hoop at some stage (pension etc.) but I will be bitterly angry.

Applying to pass through the pay threshold had not been seen as a positive process, three-quarters mentioning that it had had a negative impact on their morale, while only 5 per cent stated that they felt positive about it.

A second questionnaire was sent to 57 of the teachers in this sample who had said that they *would* apply in Round 2 and 50 responses were obtained. In 46 cases the head supported the teacher's application, while in the remaining four cases the teachers did not know. Of the 50 teachers in this sample only one teacher was *unsuccessful*. Not one single teacher, however, reported that the whole process had had any impact on their classroom practice. Over half said that it had made no impact on their morale either.

The majority of these teachers justified their action and said that applying to cross the threshold in Round 2 was the right thing to do:

> The money was nice! I accept that from the headteacher and school's point of view that it has some bearing on the *perception* of the quality of staff (if not reality?) to outside bodies such as Ofsted (we are awaiting an inspection). However, I doubt the four year olds I teach would be impressed!

> It actually went more smoothly than I had anticipated – and the money is welcome.

> I'm a hothead. I should have done it first time, but got myself into an angry froth. I deserve the money. It boosts my lump sum and pension.

Impact on classroom practice

In 2000, when the government introduced performance-related pay, it was stated to be a means of rewarding teachers for effective performance. It would have been politically difficult to award all teachers a pay increase without any conditions attached, so the assumption was that most would strive to improve their practice in order to receive their £2,000. Attaching pay increases to performance raised an expectation that improvement would occur. The evidence from our surveys of both successful and unsuccessful teachers, and indeed from headteachers, reported in Chapter 3, suggests that little change for the better occurred.

Two-thirds of teachers in the sample of those who had *successfully* crossed the threshold reported no modifications to their classroom practice. This should not be too surprising. Those judged to be meritorious naturally assume that their teaching is considered by their headteacher to be effective. Of the one-third of *successful* teachers who said the threshold assessment process had made an impact on their practice, the vast majority referred only to increased record keeping, to help them with future appraisals: 'I now keep all the bits of paper I can and write a lot more down – what a waste of time!' Even amongst those who referred to the gathering of pupil progress data, most appeared to view this solely in terms of future 'evidence', rather than as a diagnostic tool: 'I make sure I have certain facts about pupils in my own file.'

There was very little evidence of change among *unsuccessful* teachers either. Table 4.6 shows that the vast majority reported no effect or a negative impact. Only 1 per cent felt it had exerted any positive effect. Most unsuccessful teachers strongly disputed the reasons cited for their lack of success, few claiming they had been given any diagnostic assessment of their practice, or support to help them identify what and how to improve. In the follow-up

Table 4.6 The impact of threshold assessment on the classroom practice of unsuccessful teachers

Impact on classroom practice	First questionnaire (n = 146) %	Second questionnaire (n = 87) %
None	42	45
Initially negative, now none	6	5
Very little (unspecified)	6	2
A detrimental effect – emotional	40	33
Withdrawal of co-operation/extra-curricular activities	0	8
Keep more records	5	7
A positive effect	1	1

Notes: These figures do not total 100 due to rounding. First questionnaire given when results became known, second questionnaire five months later. This table does not include teachers who indicated, when completing the questionnaire(s), that they were no longer teaching.

questionnaire, given five months later, the same question was asked again, with similar results.

Comparison of the data from the original and follow-up questionnaire surveys of unsuccessful teachers shows that some responded by exacting revenge, deliberately opting out of any additional responsibilities:

> I am wholly disaffected and very angry. I now do sufficient to get by. I shall just keep the system ticking over until I reach the age when I can retire without an actuarial reduction of my pension.

> I am now far less willing to spend all the extra time and effort I previously did at the expense of my own family who saw so little of me. I try to leave school earlier and spend much less weekend time on planning sheets. I do my best for my class but do not offer to take on extras or work in my own time.

> I still work flat out for the pupils but now no longer run football and cricket clubs after school. I will not help with school fêtes. The pupils have lost out.

Conclusion

A key concern for teachers was that performance-related pay might be divisive, threatening professional and personal relationships within schools. There were also worries that some heads might be unfair in their judgements. Many teachers did not believe that linking pay to performance would raise teaching standards or have a positive impact on levels of pupil attainment. Most original fears were dispelled when only 3 per cent were unsuccessful. This minority felt isolated and stigmatised, but their number in any school was too low, usually only one or two, to cause major splits in the staffroom. Some teachers' prediction that the threshold assessment process would bring about few improvements in classroom practice, however, was generally correct.

Successful teachers, most of whom had initially viewed the procedure with suspicion and distrust, became more positive about it once they had received the financial reward. There still remained a number of concerns, especially about the bureaucracy involved, the time required and the need to furnish evidence in the form of lesson plans, pupil progress data, approving letters from parents, or evidence of organisation of school trips, as the following comments demonstrate:

> Threshold assessment has made me more conscious of recording every-thing said by anyone on the staff. I have copies of everything. I know I have achieved my performance management targets and have an overkill of paperwork to support it.

> I have regular line management meetings and keep every piece of paper to back up any claims I need to justify.

Some teachers expressed the fear that an excess of record keeping would lead them to neglect their performance in the classroom. Performance management, the second strand of the government's performance-related pay policy, discussed later in this book, requires a teacher's line manager to observe them on only one occasion during the cycle. Most teachers can stage at least one good lesson if they know they are to be observed.

Concerns were voiced by both successful and unsuccessful teachers about the inconsistency of the procedure across schools. Teachers in different schools had very different experiences. Although in many cases senior managers appeared to have handled the whole delicate issue with sensitivity and aplomb, others gave wrong information, or behaved in a crass manner. In one school a husband and wife were told that it was not possible for a married couple both to be successful, which was completely untrue. Many reservations expressed by both successful and unsuccessful teachers related to the amount of power and patronage residing with headteachers:

> I think the system is intrinsically unfair because it relies upon personal opinion to a large degree. My head had little respect for me and made this obvious on occasions. She allowed her personal opinion to affect her professional judgement. I feel more of the process should be carried out externally.

A few senior managers apparently resorted to blackmail, using their position of power to mislead less well informed members of staff:

I was put into a quandary when the acting head said that if I made an appeal [against the verdict], those who had been awarded the Threshold in my school might lose it, because I would be appealing against the 'process', not pursuing my individual claim.

When policy is translated into practice across many different types of school, intent and action are not always matched. Heads were precluded from helping teachers with their applications, yet some did in fact help, or found other ways to provide advice. When certain teachers' cases were not supported, the question arose why, if they were now deemed incompetent, no action had been taken against them previously.

This difficult situation was exacerbated when the head failed to give teachers detailed feedback on reasons for their lack of success. It was rare for heads to suggest how performance might be improved and to offer support, either in-house or externally. Perhaps they hoped their 'unsuccessful' member of staff would become disillusioned and leave. Such an alienation strategy may even have been effective. Of the 174 unsuccessful teachers completing the first questionnaire, some 50 (29 per cent) intended to leave their school. Indeed 33 of these 50 had already moved, were planning to move to another school, or were undertaking supply teaching elsewhere, while the remaining 17 had decided to quit the teaching profession altogether, some taking early retirement.

Even successful teachers reacted negatively, some stating specifically that they would not recommend their profession to newcomers:

> I have been very angry indeed about the waste of my time and my colleagues' by this process. If there is not a better way of recognising teachers' contributions and paying at European levels (e.g. as teachers are in France and Germany) and improving conditions of employment for us, I think we should all quit the profession at the earliest opportunity.

> Teaching is the most denigrated position in society – it has no status and low financial reward. I, and most of my colleagues, would actively dissuade any bright student from considering it as a career. Successive governments have made teachers the scapegoat for their own inadequate social policies. If I could leave today I would. So would 90 per cent of teachers I know in my age bracket.

> Threshold assessment will not raise standards or morale because teachers need more time to do the job rather than more money. I would rather see more teachers employed than have the £2,000. To attract quality entrants the job must become more realistic in its demands.

The message from the majority of all teachers in this study, successful or unsuccessful, was that, while additional remuneration was welcome and long overdue, all teachers should have been given an increase in pay without having to undertake a form filling exercise they perceived as flawed and vulnerable to bias. At least as important, constantly demanded by teachers and their unions, was a reduction in their workload.

5 Agents and agencies

Headteachers and teachers were at the centre of the action when performance-related pay was introduced, but they operated within a framework alongside other actors in the events: agents and agencies like headteacher and teacher unions, local education authorities, private companies brought in to offer training, and external assessors whose job it was to make sure that schools followed the rules. As we have described some of the work of assessors and trainers in earlier chapters, this account will concentrate on trade unions and local authorities, neither of whom was scheduled by the government to play a prominent role, though the unions were consulted.

Teacher unions

When systems of performance-related pay are introduced or proposed, it is often assumed that the teacher unions will prove to be difficult. As we described in Chapter 2 it has been common for performance-related pay schemes to collapse after a time, or to be withdrawn in the face of opposition at the pilot stage. Teacher union opposition has then frequently been cited as a factor in the termination or non-introduction of the scheme. Like many other trade and professional associations in the United Kingdom, teacher unions had been weakened by legislation introduced under a Conservative government in the 1980s. At the time when performance-related pay was introduced there was no strong appetite for a strike among teachers, and privately many union officers acknowledged that there was little point in trying to call one.

The perspective of each of the six associations and unions representing teachers and headteachers was sought on the whole threshold assessment process by analysing their documentation and interviewing a small sample of national and regional officials. Information about the scope and effectiveness of the unions' advice has also been reported in earlier chapters of this book, in the accounts of interviews with teachers and headteachers, and from the national questionnaire surveys of headteachers and of teachers who were judged not to have met the threshold standards. One national official from each of the six unions involved was interviewed, and there were further interviews with local and regional officers:

- Association of Teachers and Lecturers (ATL)
- National Association of Head Teachers (NAHT)
- National Association of Schoolmasters and Union of Women Teachers (NASUWT)
- National Union of Teachers (NUT)
- Professional Association of Teachers (PAT)
- Secondary Heads' Association (SHA).

The Unions' opinions of threshold assessment

National Union of Teachers

While all the unions had criticisms of various aspects of the arrangements, only the National Union of Teachers (NUT) was against the whole process of threshold assessment both in theory and practice. It was proudly pointed out in interview that the NUT had been founded in 1870 in opposition to 'payment by results' and that the union had still felt sufficiently strongly about the issue to take the government to the High Court. Their stated position was 'that every teacher should have a pay rise of £2,000 or 10 per cent, whichever is greater'.

The NUT had actually commissioned its own research into performance-related pay in schools (Richardson 1999a and 1999b), which was described in Chapter 2, and they used the findings of this to justify their opposition to the proposed scheme. The union's preference was for a flat-rate increase, and they objected to the rise being restricted to teachers at point 9 on the pay scale in operation at that time. The focus on teachers' individual contribution to their pupils' progress was especially disliked by the NUT, and they were annoyed that their objection was not accepted by the government. The national official we interviewed put it starkly, saying: 'I think it's outrageous that we're not listened to.'

The NUT actually took the government to court, early in the process, on the grounds that teachers' contractual conditions had been changed without consultation and it won a judgement which required the government to consult with the School Teachers' Review Body (STRB). Hailing this as a triumph, the NUT believed it provided the opportunity for significant changes to the threshold assessment scheme, including:

- acceptance of applications from teachers who had not previously applied;
- a formal appeals system;
- the removal of *Pupil Progress* as a separate standard;
- the removal of the decision-making powers from external assessors – leaving them as moderators and advisors;

- acknowledgement that there was no need for teachers to prepare port-folios of evidence.

After consultation, the School Teachers' Review Body recommended, and the government agreed to institute, a system of appeal or 'review' for teachers who were judged as not having met the criteria to cross the threshold and move on to a higher scale. The NUT court action caused some bitterness with the other unions and the union was criticised by them for keeping money out of the pay packets of teachers, with one interviewee saying: 'The only victor of the NUT judgement is Gordon Brown [Chancellor of the Exchequer]. Just think of all the interest the government's going to get on that money which has been allocated, while this is all sorted out.' But after a delay of several months the government's policy went ahead without other changes.

National Association of Schoolmasters and Union of Women Teachers

At the other end of the spectrum, the NASUWT had long had a policy which accepted the idea of a salary 'bar' which teachers would cross. The historic position of the NASUWT was to represent the 'career teacher' and so the idea of a 'gateway to higher salaries for classroom teachers' fits with the union's ethos. While not happy with every aspect of the government's plans – especially the linking of pay with what it called 'crude exam league tables' – a NASUWT official interviewed thought it neither could nor should campaign against a pay rise for its members:

> We felt that if the government was prepared to offer an additional £2,000 to certain groups of teachers – which in itself was then a gateway to higher salaries for classroom teachers – then what we should do is try and make sure the system was as reasonable as it was possible to be and to offer support to members who wish to volunteer to go through that process.

The union adopted the pragmatic position that negotiating with the government had produced positive results, one officer saying: 'It still was not the kind of system we would particularly like at the end of it but it was certainly better than when we started.'

Association of Teachers and Lecturers

Like the NASUWT, the ATL had a history of pressing for policies which would give more promotional opportunities for teachers who did not move on to management posts. At first this took the form of arguing for more responsibility posts but in the 1990s they were 'edging towards' payment for advanced skills. After consultation, the union found that its members were willing to accept some form of link between performance and pay, saying, in effect, 'if we can be sure it will be fair enough then we can accept it'. Once the idea of teachers who crossed the threshold having to sign a separate contract had been discarded by the government, the ATL supported the scheme, though still with some reservations.

Professional Association of Teachers

The PAT did not object to the notion of a threshold to be crossed, nor to the idea of a higher pay scale for teachers who crossed it, but it did object to the application process and the involvement of external assessors. Its view, stated by a national official in interview, was that: 'If you have in place proper performance management ... then any self-respecting headteachers would be able to say, once the teacher got to point 9, "Yes, this teacher is up to standard and therefore should progress to the upper pay points".'

The Headteachers' Unions

The perspective of the unions who represent headteachers is often quite different from that of teacher unions. The Secondary Heads' Association (SHA), whose officers are themselves mainly practising headteachers, admitted to strong differences of opinion both among its members and its Executive. They had members who welcomed the opportunity to reward teachers they thought were doing a good job, but a national officer described some of the vigorous opposition:

> There was a strong and significant minority who would have preferred to say 'let's have nothing to do with it at all' – and this was reflected as far up as Executive and Council level where decisions were made.

SHA did not officially oppose the idea of introducing a threshold to higher pay scales, believing that it would have more influence if it accepted the government's agenda and tried to bring about changes through negotiation, than if it opposed the whole idea:

> When we made our submission we tried to make it as positive and constructive as we could but, in saying that, we would not have carried all members with us.

Originally SHA favoured the idea of teachers building up a portfolio or profile which could be matched against known criteria. They were unhappy about the role of external assessors and would have preferred headteachers to have been trusted to make the decisions, within some form of external appeal system. A national official, also a practising head, found it bizarre that one form of daily patronage was simple and immediate, while the new performance-related pay version was swathed in bureaucracy:

We make decisions about people and their position and their pay every day of the week, and it seems odd that I can decide who's going to be head of English, by competitive interview – I can even, with the governors' blessing, pay out up to £5,000 to get someone to walk through the doors – but we have to have this elaborate bureaucratic process to decide whether someone's doing an effective job or not.

The National Association of Head Teachers (NAHT), which has many primary school headteachers as members, was generally unenthusiastic about the principle of performance-related pay, concerned about the way threshold assessment had been introduced and worried about the practicalities. Once it had been introduced, however, the union tried to make the best of what one national official described as 'a curate's egg' (i.e. good in parts).

Some of the teacher unions also have headteachers as members. A local NUT officer described the union's headteacher members as: 'all totally opposed to it [threshold assessment] certainly on workloads grounds ... I think they've all viewed the whole thing, without exception, with a great deal of distaste.' Interviewees from other teacher unions did not mention their headteacher members when talking about their union policy, although officers interviewed did express considerable sympathy for the extra work they had to do, such as: processing large numbers of applications, making decisions about salaries of staff, having these judgements questioned by an external assessor, and dealing with teachers who had not reached the required standard.

Training and advice

The unions identified two different client groups for the advice and training they had given on threshold assessment – the unions' own representatives and officers, and their ordinary members. Although headteachers had been very critical of their training for the process, they did not appear to rely heavily on their unions for advice to fill the gap. Teachers, on the other hand, were not given any training, though they received documentation and could access the government's website. Their support and advice came from a variety of other sources, including in-service training days and 'trickle down' training from their heads, so they regarded the advice they received from their unions as important and valuable.

Information and advice from the unions were provided in a variety of forms. General information was given in briefings and newsletters and on websites, while individual telephone advice was used extensively. The head-teachers' unions concentrated mainly on problems which might arise, such as borderline cases, or applications from teachers who had been absent, while the teachers' unions gave basic information about how to fill in the application forms and advice about eligibility. Some teacher unions, such as the ATL, even provided 'model answers' for their members, while others gave more general advice.

Problems and queries

Despite the general advice and information they gave, all the unions received many individual requests for help. Many heads were dissatisfied with their training, so both headteachers' unions had members who were worried about making judgements against the standards. An officer of the NAHT said that heads were unsure, in the early stages, whether they were looking for 'good' teachers or merely 'satisfactory' ones, and an SHA officer questioned whether they really were dealing with 'standards' rather than statements of good practice, as they did not have any basis for measurement.

Teacher union officers mentioned receiving a number of political or philosophical questions about the principle of performance-related pay and the union's position on it. Most of the problems encountered, however, were practical. The NASUWT received so many similar questions early on, that they based a section of their own information booklet on them. Called 'Dispelling the Myths', this section answered the common questions about how many people were expected to cross the threshold, who was entitled to apply, whether school governors would be involved in making the decisions and whether teachers were expected to collect portfolios of evidence.

According to Murnane and Cohen (1986), one of the common factors in successful performance-related pay schemes for teachers was that the teachers had to produce evidence and documentation to prove their suitability. Gathering evidence, however, was not viewed favourably by many of the teachers who contacted their unions, though perhaps this was because the other criteria for successful schemes, such as teacher involvement, being made to feel special, a low-profile scheme and schools being located in affluent areas, were not present either. Concern about the *quantity* of evidence required was expressed by many teachers telephoning their unions for help and the unions were keen to reassure them:

> There was an assumption that a great mountain of – shopping trolleys full of – exercise books and planning and departmental meetings and keystage meetings would have to be provided, so we put people right on that.
>
> (PAT)

Queries about what counted as evidence for particular standards were also common. An ATL officer reported questions about producing evidence on pupil progress, particularly from members who taught children with special educational needs who did not realise that their own records of progress were as valid as public examination results.

While most enquiries were factual and, apart from the volume, relatively easy to deal with, many local teacher union officers also found themselves being asked to give emotional support to their members, as one explained:

I had one person who said 'Can I just come round and can you go through the form with me?' That was the sort of state people were in and there were people ringing up ... and asking if they could go down to the office ... and we actually said 'No' because we weren't prepared to actually sit and do that for people. I gave the Teacher Support Network number to some people because I don't do counselling.

(NUT)

Most irksome to union officers were irritatingly trivial questions from some members who were overly dependent on the judgement of others about matters they could have easily decided for themselves:

There were people ... who asked whether they should staple or paper clip it!

(NASUWT)

The standards

Both headteacher and teacher union officers queried the use of the word 'standards' in the assessment process, with its implications of measurability:

They're not *standards*. As 'statements of good practice' they are hard to disagree with.

(SHA)

Of course teachers should be involved in their continuing professional development, teachers should be participating in the ethos of the school. Of course teachers should be planning lessons in terms of groups of children and individual children. Of course teachers should be doing what they can to progress pupils' standards. But it's the conversion of that into something measurable, something quantifiable ... How is it possible to measure a teacher's general contribution to school ethos?

(PAT)

Several union officers identified the *Pupil Progress* standard as 'the one causing most angst' (NASUWT). A headteacher union officer spoke of his union's 'grave reservations' while a teacher union officer described the decision to use pupil progress in a quantitative way as 'a recipe for disaster'. The major problem was seen as ascribing progress to one particular teacher, especially in secondary schools. Nonetheless, all the unions considered that they had been consulted about the standards and that the government had made alterations in the light of their representations. This did not mean, however, that they were entirely happy with the end result, which one officer described as 'just far too many hoops to jump through'.

Despite their reservations about the standards, the unions had confidence in their members' ability to meet them, especially once the climate changed and they realised that the vast majority of teachers were expected to be successful. With a degree of cynicism a headteacher union officer pointed out:

> It did not take a genius to look at the amount of money that had been set aside for the process and the number of teachers, to work out that there was enough to put them all through! You also asked, in an election year, what was going to be the message if it went back that 50 per cent of the teachers were not effective!

Headteachers' ability to judge the standards

Although they represented different constituencies, both heads' and teachers' unions agreed that most heads would be able to judge adequately their teachers' ability to reach the standards. The heads' unions were most concerned about the difficulties their members would face with teachers on the borderline. Teacher unions felt that the two problems standing in the way of some heads doing the job properly were shortage of time and the need to be acknowledged as an expert teacher 'whose judgement is based on his own experience and whose judgement is respected because they're the expert teacher'.

Teacher union officers believed the process gave heads too much power and cited instances of the unprofessional way in which some heads had conducted themselves:

> We've had so much misinformation given out by headteachers about the whole process ... Ridiculous things – people being told 'don't bother to apply, you won't get it'. People also being told, you know, encouraged, told 'you must apply – I'll give it to you' and this sort of thing, which was terrible ... By far the nastiest aspect of it from a casework point of view, was the innuendo and the kind of threats that people felt, you know – 'If you're not able to do this work then I'm not going to able to support your threshold application.'

> For some schools the process was much more straightforward because there was a system of monitoring in the school. In others the heads were not equipped to cope with it because they had not done any monitoring and they had no evidence to show. There was a crop of schools where heads suddenly decided to do classroom observation which was ridiculous because it all had to pre-date the application date.

External assessors were mentioned as important safeguards against possible bias and as an insurance that headteachers did their job the way that they should:

I do believe that some headteachers did take the opportunity to give biased opinions against teachers for a variety of reasons. Having said that, I think the majority of headteachers strove to do the job professionally but I do think that their attention was focused on it much better by the presence of external assessment. I am quite convinced that if there had not been an external assessment process, the work that heads did in many more schools would not have been as rigorous as it should have been.

Governors

Given the key part they play in many aspects of school administration, including setting performance management targets for heads, it might seem strange that school governors had no role in the threshold assessment process. This, however, according to union interviewees, is how it should be. They showed no enthusiasm for the involvement of governors at any stage of the process, doubting their competence and worrying about confidentiality:

I think they're finding it difficult enough already for the assessment of the headteacher's performance.

(NASUWT)

No [governors should not be involved]. It could create terrible problems for us – governors who are not professionals ... making judgements about teachers' professional competence. And there are also major issues for us about confidentiality.

(NUT)

Working with the private sector

Interviewees were not asked specifically about the role of the private firm responsible for the deployment and management of external assessors, Cambridge Education Associates Ltd (CEA), but several volunteered opinions, which were mostly favourable, though one NUT officer was politically opposed to private companies' participation in the exercise:

It's like a lot of this Government's education policies. They are Tory education policies that I was hoping this Government would have actually stopped, but in fact they seem to have gone further down the line of privatisation and putting things out to private contracts and that's what Cambridge Education Associates are really.

(NUT)

The NUT and other unions, however, reported that they had good relationships with Cambridge Education Associates nationally and could go to them with queries and concerns. The ATL and NAHT found this useful when problems arose with assessors:

> It was really very helpful, very effective that CEA had built contact with us. We've had very good access to the assessors' senior managers ... and CEA have also copied us in, very helpfully to their own guidance notes to assessors so we can quote that stuff back to them.
>
> (ATL)

> There was a problem over amount of evidence assessors' are asking for ... We addressed that and the CEA then asked assessors to only ask for what's needed.
>
> (NAHT)

NASUWT also valued the contact they had with CEA, particularly the fact that they were able to attend the training sessions for assessors and receive all information:

> We were very fortunate in that the people who manage CEA recognise the importance of good relationships with the teacher unions. What we tended to do is liaise with them about how they would conduct the process ... We do not believe threshold would have worked had it not been for ourselves and CEA. It would not have worked if it had been left with the DfEE.
>
> (NASUWT)

After the verdict

The review process

All the teacher unions had argued for an appeals process but, of those representing headteachers, an NAHT representative described the agreed process as 'terrible' while SHA thought it was:

> Totally unnecessary! We feel you either have a headteacher judgement with a proper review or appeals procedure or the headteacher judgement with threshold assessor. There must be some recourse to appeal, independent review, whatever, but we thought that was what the threshold assessor was.
>
> (SHA)

Teacher unions had pressed for, and in the case of the NUT gone to court for, the right of members to appeal against an unsuccessful result of their application. The ATL believed that the government would have been vulnerable to court action by aggrieved teachers:

We always argued that the DfEE would be wrong in law, that it couldn't be final. We could always go for a tribunal, we could always go to the High Court. The cases that could travel that far wouldn't be all the cases in which people felt unfairness had occurred, but the DfEE was factually and legally wrong all the way through, and that the assessor's judgement could not be final.

(ATL)

Unsuccessful teachers who were union representatives

The anticipated percentage of teachers who would pass the threshold increased as the process progressed, as we have reported earlier in this book, and by the time the results came through it was over 97 per cent of the eligible teachers who applied. Though pleased in many ways, the teachers' unions found the high success rate caused some problems, particularly the isolation felt by their few unsuccessful members. Headteacher union officers believed the failures were mainly poor practitioners, but this was contested by teacher union officers.

Representatives of all the teacher unions argued that the system was biased against 'non-standard' teachers, as was reported in Chapter 4. These were people like supply teachers, home tutors and part-timers, who did not fit neatly into the categories of secondary subject teacher or primary class teacher. Their union was often the only source of help and advice available to them. But there was even deeper concern about what some officers believed was bias against their own school-based union representatives. One NASUWT official was convinced that such representatives were suffering for their trade union activities:

We are getting the feeling that teacher union representatives are over-represented [in the number failing to cross the threshold to higher pay scales], and we understand that is common. The NUT have had the same experience, with two levels of over-representation: first in the sample [of teachers scrutinised by the external assessor] and then, apparently, in the 'standards not met' [group].

(NASUWT)

The ATL claimed to have noticed a similar pattern and cited an example of one school in which the only unsuccessful teachers were the three NUT, NASUWT and ATL representatives. There could be other explanations for such failures. It could be that some teachers who suspected they might have problems deliberately signed up as their union representative, to be in a better position to fight their case; or the headteacher may have felt that normal duties were being neglected because of union activities. Equally it could be that the fears of the unions were justified, and some heads did indeed take the opportunity to settle old scores with their local adversary.

Local education authorities

Whereas local authorities had played a key role in teacher appraisal in the 1990s (Haynes 1996), being given responsibility for training and expected to engage in close supervision of its implementation, they were effectively excluded from the performance-related pay initiative. Private agencies provided training of headteachers and external assessors and communication was most frequently directly between government and schools. It was a sharp contrast, brought about within a decade, underlining the greatly reduced role in policy implementation of the 150 local education authorities (LEAs) in England.

Despite their effectively having been written out of the script, we decided to contact a number of them to see if they did actually play, or indeed desire, any role in the process, given that they still carried significant responsibility for the quality of teaching and learning in the schools in their area. A questionnaire was constructed containing a mix of closed and open questions, through which we sought to discover their experiences of and their position on performance-related pay. LEAs were not required to identify themselves but they were asked to indicate which category of authority they were. Forty-five LEAs (30 per cent) completed and returned the questionnaire (13 County Councils, 17 Unitary Authorities, 7 Metropolitan Districts, 7 London Boroughs and 1 District Council). It was clear from their responses that they played virtually no part in threshold assessment, but some did fashion a role for themselves in the performance management part of the process.

Documentation and training

Forty of the 45 LEAs indicated that they had provided, or were providing some sort of documentation relating to teachers' performance-related pay to their local schools, mainly for heads and governors. The responses indicated four main types of materials:

- A model performance management policy
- Updates about the procedure
- Advice specific to the higher pay scale (upper pay spine 2)
- General 'guidance' (no details given).

A small number of LEAs also mentioned other forms of advice: 'notes for team leaders'; 'notes for teachers'; 'checklists for headteachers and governors'; and materials setting out 'exemplar objective setting'.

Only two LEAs indicated that they had not been involved at all with providing any kind of training. The training offered by the other 43 concentrated mainly on raising awareness and setting performance management objectives. In some cases external consultants had been engaged to run the training. It is interesting that lesson observation was also a common topic in training sessions. Our data from case studies to be described in Chapters 7 and 8 indicate that observation specifically related to teachers' performance management objectives was rare.

Almost all of the LEAs (43 out of 45) reported that they had been contacted by headteachers about aspects of implementing performance management in their school. The most common query was for help with potential thorny internal relationships issues, such as the criteria for deciding who should proceed to higher pay scales. Enquiries about funding performance-related pay, timescales, objective setting, assessment and resolving disputes with teachers, were also common, this occurring in 50–90 per cent of LEAs.

LEAs were also invited to indicate what role, if any, they felt LEAs *should* have in the performance management procedure. No majority view emerged in the responses to this question. This may have been because many were short of cash, so they would not actively seek additional roles without matching resources. However, a large minority believed that LEAs should be responsible for regularly auditing the implementation of the procedure, while some felt they could provide useful guidance on linking teachers' objectives with schools' planning. Only a small number felt strongly that LEAs should have a prominent position:

> [We need] a statement from the Department for Education and Skills to say LEAs are key players!

> The LEA should play the leading role. Officers can work with heads, governors and professional associations to secure an effective performance management policy which links together LEA improvement plans, school improvement plans and objectives for individual members of staff.

It was difficult to obtain any sense of the extent to which performance management was being implemented in a particular region, especially when there was no role for local government. Nonetheless a specific question was asked to discover whether any formal evaluation was being undertaken by the LEA of the implementation of performance management in its schools. Over half of LEAs (24 out of 45) felt able to give an estimate of the percentage of their schools where performance management was believed to have taken root. The estimate averaged at 71 per cent of schools, though the range in different LEAs was from 40 per cent to 90 per cent. This figure must, of course, be interpreted cautiously, as it is based on estimation, rather than on formal and systematic evaluation.

Local authority perspectives on performance-related pay

Not surprisingly, since they were operating at the margins of the process, LEA respondents were more likely to cite disadvantages than advantages.

Twenty-eight of the 45 LEAs identified one or more disadvantages, the most common being lack of criteria and uncertainty surrounding funding for the higher pay scales, and the workload imposed by performance management. Although two-thirds said they would like to see modifications to the government's model, there was no consensus as to what these changes should be.

The evidence from this part of our research suggests that, although there was no formal place for them, some LEAs did try to become involved. The most detached response was from those that said they did nothing, seeing it as outside their remit. At the other extreme, one LEA reported that it had (a) set up an advisory group which included representatives from the LEA, all the teacher unions and the diocesan boards of education, (b) funded two day residential courses for new team leaders and one day courses for new teachers, and (c) provided half day sessions for headteachers on enhancing the way they conducted performance management. This same LEA had also been at the forefront of providing support when we studied teacher appraisal in 1992–4, and the responses of its officer (who voluntarily identified his LEA) show that the 1990s initiatives had been sustained in its schools since their inception, as the LEA continued to believe it should give a lead to its schools. Its 1992 'Appraisal Team', set up to oversee that procedure, had been renamed 'Performance Management and Review Team'.

The supporting cast

The introduction of performance-related pay was like no other precedent of its kind in England in the preceding century. Until the 1980s there were few examples on government policy making any impact on individual teachers' pay, other than to approve recommendations about national salary scales which might include special allowances for those carrying additional responsibility. Most policy decisions at national level progressed to schools via local authorities. In many cases teacher unions were closely involved, sometimes positively, on other occasions in a blocking or amending role. Private companies played no part at all, other than as suppliers of books or materials.

The performance-related pay process was radically different for the agents and agencies that had once been central in new developments. Local authorities had no formal role at all, though some fashioned one. Teacher unions settled for small gains, triumphant if their suggestions made an impact at the edges, mitigating something they believed was harsh or inappropriate. 'Official' training and external assessment were provided by private companies, rather than local authorities, though some of the latter tried to fill gaps, humanise what they saw as a mechanical process, offer advice, or exert influence.

Ironically, although it marginalised them, the process often brought former adversaries – the unions and the LEAs – closer together in their adversity, some union officers even lamenting the passage of the days when they negotiated directly together on matters affecting their members' pay and conditions. While not always over-enthusiastic about the privatisation of such elements as training and external assessment, the unions showed no great hostility to the private companies providing these. All these changed relationships, procedures and roles would have looked strange to anyone who had been abroad for the previous ten years. In terms of implementation, the differences between the introduction of formal teacher appraisal in the early 1990s, and performance-related pay and performance management a decade later, were substantial. Part III will explore in detail the implementation of performance management.

Part III
Performance management

6 Performance management in schools

The headteacher's perspective

Once the first round of the *threshold assessment* procedure had been implemented, and those teachers had been identified who were to be allowed to progress to the higher pay scale (the upper pay spine), schools were expected to move on to the second phase of the government's performance-related pay strategy, *performance management*. This was to be the keystone of the overall policy, because it was intended to become a permanent feature, a form of management which would take root in schools and become an organic part of their day-to-day running, not just a short-term piece of ephemera, or the means of offering a one-off pay rise. Headteachers would, in future, manage the performance of their colleagues through regular appraisals. Those who had progressed through the threshold to a higher scale would be eligible to rise through this upper pay spine, thereby earning, from time to time, further increments of around £1,000.

Schools were asked to introduce performance management within either a nine-month or an eighteen-month timescale. Many schools felt they already had good forms of such management in place, so the shorter period of nine months often appealed, though some complained that the 'official' version of performance management was not as effective as their existing procedures. Others were faced with a great deal of work initiating the whole process in accordance with the principles under which it was intended to operate.

As is usually the case when a mass initiative is introduced, the actualities of it are well worth studying. In theory, schools have a set of procedures they are required to follow and all should be implementing the processes in the form laid down. It has been our experience in previous research projects, however, that intent and action are not universally matched. While some introduce externally-imposed policies almost to the letter, others amend the process and shape it to their local conditions and context, or even distort it considerably, sometimes to the point where the original formulation is barely discernible. In certain cases people do not implement the policy at all.

We were curious to know, therefore, what was going to happen in the case of performance management, a particularly determined government intervention in the internal running of schools, and one that was tied to teachers' pay. There were no hypotheses in advance about exactly how matters would proceed, because mixed feelings had been expressed by key players like headteachers. In any case, some participants in an action can proclaim hostility, then implement something faithfully. The obverse of this may also occur, with initial supporters failing to match their enthusiasm with appropriate action.

The situation invited close scrutiny, not only from outside, but from inside the school. We decided, therefore, to collect information at a national and local level. The first strategy was to conduct another large-scale survey of headteachers' views and experiences, as they implemented this second and crucial stage of the performance-related pay strategy. Areas to be investigated included: how the policy was actually implemented, what team leaders did, the setting of objectives, lesson observation and feedback, the measurement of pupil progress, how the process was linked with decisions about pay, perceived advantages and disadvantages, and modifications made to procedures in the light of experience.

Related to this was a sharp focus, within our intensive case studies of primary and secondary teachers and schools, on what was actually happening on the ground. It is the first part of this analysis, the headteacher survey, which is reported in this present chapter. The second part is described in Chapters 7 and 8, which relate to the experiences of individual teachers.

Headteachers who responded to the questionnaire

The means of sampling was the same as for the headteacher questionnaire on threshold assessment described in Chapter 3, but the actual sample is different. There are many more primary schools than secondary schools, so the questionnaire was sent to a stratified random sample of one in fourteen primary and middle school headteachers and one out of three secondary headteachers in schools in England, as happened with the earlier survey. Respondents are in any case anonymous, so it was not possible to conduct a direct one-to-one comparison on items that were common to both questionnaires, only grouped data can be analysed. Anonymity is an important part of surveys such as this, as we felt that it was important for heads to be able to speak freely. It has been our experience that heads feel themselves to be vulnerable in a 'high stakes' system, where they may easily be blamed if their school performs badly, so anonymity seems wiser than identification for written responses such as this survey.

Once again a sizeable sample was obtained, with 1,102 questionnaires being returned by headteachers, a 47 per cent return rate. This is very high for a mailed questionnaire, especially given that many heads were boycotting all non-compulsory paperwork at the time, in protest at the large amount of bureaucracy with which they had to contend. The number of years spent as a headteacher is displayed in Table 6.1, which shows that the heads were evenly spread, with about 20 per cent of the sample in each of the five bands of time. A one-third sample of the questionnaires was selected for analysis of the responses to open questions.

Over three-quarters of the heads (78 per cent) had been head of their current school at the time performance management was introduced in September 2000. The respondents were heads of a range of schools, within a wide geographical area covering every one of the 150 local authorities in England. Table 6.2 shows the type of school of which they were head and this illustrates a 60:40 primary to secondary ratio.

Training for performance management

Whereas heads had been extremely critical of the training they had received for the threshold assessment procedure, in the case of performance management nearly half were satisfied with their training, 44 per cent were not and 8 per cent had not undertaken training. The same failings were identified by those who were critical of it: trainers appeared poorly briefed and were sometimes patronising; there was a 'one size fits all' approach, which did not take account of the individual circumstances of schools, and this was seen as unhelpful; the format of the training sessions had been too rigidly prescribed, with little opportunity for heads to ask questions; and there was no attempt to discuss what procedures would be in place to consider how teachers should progress along the upper pay spine. There was also evidence that some who had become heads since the original sessions were undertaken, had received no training in the implementation of performance management.

One secondary head commented wryly on the small amount of training provided: 'The single largest performance management system was introduced

Table 6.1 How many years have you been a headteacher?

	Years as headteacher %	Years as headteacher at current school %
3 years or less	18	35
4–7 years	22	29
8–11 years	18	16
12–15 years	22	13
16+ years	21	8

Table 6.2 Of which type of school are you headteacher?

School type	Percentage
Infant or First	2.0
Junior or Middle	7.0
Primary or Combined First and Middle	51.0
Secondary	39.0
Special	0.1
Other	0.2

Note: These figures do not total 100 due to rounding.

within what was half a day!' These negative feelings about the training may have influenced the 16 per cent of heads who responded that they had not felt very informed about performance management when they implemented it in their school. The majority (54 per cent) felt 'quite informed', however, and 30 per cent of cases actually felt 'well informed'.

Implementation

Timescale

For the first cycle of the performance management procedure, schools were asked to choose either a nine-month or an eighteen-month cycle. There was a near fifty-fifty split, with 54 per cent opting for the longer period, and the remainder (46 per cent) choosing the shorter cycle. Although schools were themselves able to select the length of cycle to suit their individual circumstances, slippage still occurred in 17 per cent of the 1,102 schools. Analysis of the qualitative data provided on the questionnaires by heads whose schools had failed to keep within their selected timescales identified three main obstacles which prevented them from keeping to schedule: staff illness; staff turnover, particularly among middle and senior managers; and the workload for Ofsted inspections, which meant that areas of teachers' work perceived as less important were neglected during that time.

Two years after the process had been initiated, the performance management procedure was fully operational in the great majority of schools (90 per cent). There was huge variation, however. By the time some schools had reached their third cycle, others had not even started. In eight schools the procedure had not been implemented at all, and in 98 cases, nearly 10 per cent, they had not reached the end of the first cycle. Half the schools had completed the first cycle and were already into the second, and in 40 per cent of cases they were into their third cycle.

It was interesting to note how schools had decided to set about the process. Each teacher had been given a 'team leader', the person, usually the teacher's line manager, who was supposed to be responsible for the day-to-day supervision of what the teacher did. Almost all heads (97 per cent) reported that a planning meeting between the teacher and team leader was the means of identifying the teacher's objectives and professional development needs. In virtually every school (98 per cent) heads stated that lesson observations were undertaken and feedback was offered, mostly (89 per cent) on a standard school lesson observation sheet. There was similar uniformity in the use of standard school performance management forms for recording objectives, used in 92 per cent of cases, while 99 per cent of schools held review meetings to assess whether objectives had been met and to set new ones for the next cycle. There was less homogeneity in some of the other aspects of the process:

- 88 per cent collected pupil performance data;
- 74 per cent held informal meetings between teacher and team leader to check on progress;
- 60 per cent undertook statistical calculation of 'value added' pupil achievement data;
- 42 per cent held a formal mid-cycle meeting between teacher and team leader to check progress.

The team leader

The approach to pairing team leader and teacher varied between schools, although 59 per cent designated the most appropriate line manager. While teachers were able to ask for a different team leader if they were unhappy with the one assigned to them in many schools, nearly a third (31 per cent) of heads indicated that there was no choice and that they simply assigned a team leader. The training of team leaders was equally varied. In the three key areas of (1) setting objectives, (2) observing lessons and (3) assessing whether or not the teacher had met their objectives, not all team leaders had received training, as Table 6.3 reveals. The figures in the columns indicate the percentages of headteachers ticking each option.

Decisions about what an individual teacher's objectives should be were usually joint decisions between the teacher and the team leader. In 9 per cent of cases it was the individual teacher's decision and in a further 9 per cent of cases it was a decision taken by the senior management of the school. In 6 per cent of cases the headteacher was the main decision-maker:

> As head I look at draft objectives with the team leader and suggest refinements where they are unspecific or too woolly.

In 5 per cent of cases the team leader was the principal determinant:

> Team leader is there to help and make suggestions.

> Team leader can impose targets if absolutely necessary. Teacher can make a written comment regarding them.

Table 6.3 Training received by team leaders

	All team leaders %	Some team leaders %	None %
1 Setting objectives	62	30	8
2 Observing lessons	57	33	10
3 Assessing whether the teacher has met objectives	47	33	20

Only occasionally were middle managers other than the team leader involved.

Objectives

The majority of heads (83 per cent) claimed to provide some form of guidance to their teachers on the nature of the objectives which should be set, though some heads who were new to the school did not give any such advice. In certain cases this was simply to make clear the broad areas which should be covered, such as pupil progress, pastoral responsibilities, professional development, or an objective linked to a subject specialism. Many heads, however, gave more specific guidance to teachers about the content of their objectives, most frequently to ensure that these fitted in with the school's action plan, school improvement plan or inspection requirements:

> We work jointly on some suggestions for whole school objectives that can be tailored, if necessary, for individuals. However, there is always space for at least one personal objective.

> The whole staff discuss and agree one whole school objective e.g. writing/ reading targets. Then each member of staff and team leader personalise it as appropriate.

> The teaching staff collectively decide common objectives for pupil progress and professional development matched to the school improvement plan. The job related objective is decided on discussion between teacher and team leader.

> One target is common to all staff but the other two are agreed by team leader and teacher.

Despite using the language of joint decision-making, however, the fact that they had ticked the box saying that they *personally* gave guidance (rather than saying 'No, we decide this jointly'), suggests that this was, in fact, a decision led by the head. Other heads were even more proactive, making specific suggestions or proposing modifications, like the secondary head who stated: 'I review objectives for suitability at the end of the review process and have asked for some to be changed'. Very few mentioned the link between objectives and pay, an exception being the head who said:

> I strongly recommend that objectives in at least two cases related directly to the school improvement plan . . . The closer they are (and the more explicit), the easier it will be for me regarding the upper pay spine.

The school's development or improvement plan was often mentioned, as heads sought to harmonise teachers' individual objectives with it. Indeed, over two-thirds (68 per cent) of respondents indicated that *all* their teachers had at least one objective linked to the school plan, while 24 per cent suggested that *most* of their teachers did.

Since the DfES required teachers to include a *Pupil Progress* objective, it is not surprising that 86 per cent of heads claimed that all of their teachers had made this a specific objective, though the means of achieving it were different. When asked what methods they used to evaluate pupil progress, headteachers' responses varied considerably in the amount of detail given and the type of comment. Some heads simply wrote 'a variety'. Many indicated the specific types of tests or public examinations used, while others talked about externally produced data sent to the school by the government and its agencies, or software packages for calculating 'value added' scores.

There were few surprises. Standard Assessment Tests were overwhelmingly the main source of data for information about pupil performance in primary schools. Almost a third of primary schools said they made use of 'teacher assessment', but only 7 per cent of secondary schools mentioned this. In this phase, the emphasis was very firmly on the results from public examinations taken at the ages of 14, 16 and beyond. Secondary schools were also more likely than primary to be undertaking 'value added' calculations for the purposes of assessing teachers' performance.

Two-thirds (66 per cent) of schools indicated that they undertook 'value added' calculations to measure pupil progress for performance management purposes. Heads were asked to provide information on how these 'value added' calculations were undertaken. Some simply said they used various externally provided packages, while others gave a little more detail as the comments below illustrate:

Primary:

> It depends on what the teacher's objective is. But if we were looking at [the] 10 per cent lowest achieving boys, for example, we would look at baseline [school entry test], previous test results etc. to measure achievement, i.e. not just concentrate on attainment.

> [For example, we give a] spelling test in September/October; same test again in June.

> In English and Maths pupil progress is measured by average points score increase over academic year.

Secondary:

> Team leaders calculate each year the 'value added' of groups of students taught by individual staff.

Spreadsheets show minimum target grade based on prior attainment and points value for whole teacher group compared with actual grades and points value for whole group. Averages are taken and difference represents progression.

We consider baseline assessment ... and set targets based on prior attainment. These are challenging but realistic and we measure outcomes against prior attainment.

Most heads believed they had some degree of control over the objectives set, 85 per cent stating that they personally saw *all* the objectives of their teachers, while 10 per cent saw the objectives of *some* of their teachers. It was only in 4 per cent of cases that heads said they did not personally see the objectives.

Problems with objective setting

The objective setting process could be problematic and a third of heads described difficulties encountered with this part of the process, the most common being objectives that were not specific, ambitious or rigorous enough. One secondary head said:

We were told by our advisor that some targets were too soft and non-specific. We had a meeting of the team leaders and tried to beef them up.

A few heads had the opposite problem, finding that the importance being given to objectives was getting out of proportion, over-ambitious targets were being set, or the issue was being approached in a mechanistic fashion. One primary head said, 'We have needed to stress to those who were anxious, that the important issue is to know why things have or have not happened – not just to have met the target.' Another outlined the delicate judgements to be made 'ensuring their objectives are challenging but achievable, without being overwhelming or too easy. It is difficult to achieve the balance.' As many schools were well into their second or third cycle, some respondents were in a position to report that objective-setting had improved, with initial problems being overcome.

Staff hostility or anxiety caused some problems. In one case the resistance was due to teachers having been given union advice to accept only three targets and not to agree to any based on percentage pupil progress data, but usually unions were not mentioned. Sometimes only one teacher was involved, but in other cases the problem seemed more pervasive. One head commented: 'Some staff have been belligerent with team leaders when lesson observation feedback has involved criticism (even when only minor).' Resistance was linked to the pupil progress objective for one secondary head who said 'Still much resistance from teachers, though they happily forecast UCAS [university entry] grades. Middle managers resist setting "value added" [targets] for the year group and only want to be responsible for their own class.'

Other problems with team leaders were identified: an occasional personality clash between teacher and team leader or, more frequently, through a team leader's inexperience. One primary head believed the difficulty for people in the middle of the school hierarchy was handling a more deliberate and sculptured style of management: 'Some team leaders have been inexpert in objective setting and this has led to some inconsistency even with the head's oversight. Some have found the transition to more pointed "management" status very difficult.' The need for consistency was mentioned by several heads, a secondary head commenting on the 'variety between individuals in terms of rigour and "hardness" of targets'.

Staff and pupil absences and changes inevitably caused difficulty, as did lack of time and money. These were frequently linked, particularly in primary schools, because money was needed to pay for cover of team leaders' classes so they could have the time they needed to set and review objectives. Also linked to the problem of lack of time were delays or changes of priority occasioned by other demands, like an Ofsted inspection or other external review.

Few heads mentioned salary issues in relation to problems associated with setting objectives, but one primary head said, 'teachers are still anxious [about] pupil progress targets, as failure to meet these could cause problems if they are on the upper pay spine, or they perceive this as so'. Some teachers were thought to be setting themselves objectives that would be attained with ease. A secondary head observed, 'the advent of performance-related pay has sharpened the process and is leading to requests for "defensive" objectives'. A new primary head, joining the school after objectives had already been set under the previous head, complained that some teachers expected to progress up the higher pay scale despite their objectives being weak, easily attainable and failing to address any aspect of school or teacher development.

Planning meetings, review meetings, lesson observations and feedback

The use of time is frequently an issue in schools. There was some variation in how schools allocated it to performance management and when staff were given the opportunity to hold their planning or review meeting. Table 6.4 shows how schools timed these meetings.

Most heads sought to provide time during the normal school day for teachers to undertake this part of the process, but in 8 per cent of cases it had to be fitted in before or after school or during the lunch hour.

Lesson observation

The observation of lessons has become more commonplace in schools, and in the period 1992–4, when the government required that all teachers had

Table 6.4 What happened in schools for planning/review meetings

When the meeting took place	Percentage
During an in-service day/twilight session	21
During normal non-contact time for both teacher and team leader	15
During non-contact time for either the teacher or team leader and cover is provided for the person without non-contact time	18
Cover is provided for both teacher and team leader so that the meeting can be held during normal contact time	26
Before school starts, at lunchtime or after school	8
A mixture of the above	10
Other	2

to be appraised, it was laid down that they had to be observed teaching on two occasions. Performance management did not require two lesson observations, however, and teacher unions had been particularly anxious to minimise the observation of teachers at work in their classroom. As a result the majority of schools (60 per cent) undertook only one observation of each teacher, while about a quarter (28 per cent) undertook two. Only in about one school in ten were there three or more observations. At the other extreme there was no lesson observation at all in 1 per cent of schools.

It was almost always (92 per cent) the team leader who did the lesson observation, though in about a quarter of schools the head or other middle and senior managers joined in. In most cases feedback was given to teachers. Table 6.5 shows the timing and nature of the feedback given. As is to be expected, verbal comments were likely to be offered immediately, or soon after the lesson, whereas written observations took longer. The caveat about Table 6.5 is that it is based on heads' perceptions. In our large-scale study of teacher appraisal in the mid-1990s (Wragg *et al.* 1996) we found that teachers reported a slower timescale for feedback than that estimated by their senior managers. On the surface, at any rate, the times given in Table 6.5 are quicker than the 1990s equivalent, when only about half of teachers were given feedback in 24 hours or less.

Reviewing the evidence

The review meetings are an opportunity to decide whether or not teachers have met their objectives. Most heads were able to cite long lists of different types of evidence:

> The types of evidence are wide ranging e.g. schemes of work, policy documents, records of meetings, evaluation by students, surveys of parents/students, school value-added analysis reports, web site designed,

Table 6.5 Timing of observation feedback

	Verbal %	Written %
Immediately after the lesson	42	4
Within 24 hours	40	32
Within 48 hours	9	22
Within one week	5	29
Different time period	1	3
Don't know	1	2
Not applicable – this type of feedback not given	1	6
No observations undertaken	1	1

Note: These figures do not always total 100 due to rounding.

course certifications, results of interview discussions with students, character of marking comments on students' work, presentations to governors, running effective field courses etc.

For the *Pupil Progress* objective, schools used a range of standardised tests and examinations depending on the age of the children. Other 'evidence' listed often included the teacher's professional development portfolio or evidence of in-service training, lesson observations and samples of children's work. Also mentioned, though less frequently, were teachers' lesson plans, reports from other staff, and, where appropriate, from Ofsted, teachers' own self-assessment forms and presentations, or what the teachers said during discussions with their team leaders. Children's work and interviews with them were much more frequently mentioned by primary heads, as were lesson plans or records, while secondary heads were slightly more likely to rely on reports or feedback from senior management.

MEETING OBJECTIVES

Some heads recognised that improvements were needed in the way objectives were assessed, with one admitting:

> We did not get this right. It was largely discussion-led, with no obligation on teachers to produce evidence to support their self-evaluation. Next time teachers will be expected to produce supportive evidence, particularly on pupil progress.

In around two-thirds of cases it was teachers, in discussion with their team leader, who decided whether their objectives had been met. In 17 per cent of cases it was the sole decision of the team leader. In less than 1 per cent of cases was the decision entirely that of the teacher involved.

Not all teachers were successful in meeting all of their objectives and in 54 per cent of cases heads had teachers who had not been successful in meeting objectives. In the vast majority of cases there would be a discussion between the teacher and team leader to explore the reasons for this. More rarely this was followed by a discussion between the teacher and another line manager or the head:

> A professional debate takes place to determine why. Was there a good reason? Were the targets inappropriate?

> Discussion takes place as to the reasons why objectives have not been met.

Often progress towards meeting the objective was noted and sometimes this was considered as important as meeting the objective:

> We place more emphasis on progress rather than total achievement.

> It's normally a case that *some* progress has been made towards the objective, so it's retained for the next cycle.

> They are asked to provide a reason BUT our aim is to set 'challenging' objectives so failure to totally meet them does not signify 'failure'.

Circumstances change during a year, so in some cases it was decided that a particular objective was no longer appropriate, something else had taken higher priority, or simply that various factors, like absence, had occurred to prevent success:

> If these have been frustrated for some reason they are re-incorporated, if still valid, without further consideration.

Objectives were flexible. They might be modified or incorporated into the following year's objectives and, if necessary, support was given and professional development considered. Stronger action was mentioned by a minority of heads who considered closer monitoring or the initiation of disciplinary action for those who appeared not to be meeting appropriate levels of competence:

> I would see continual failure to be a cause for competency procedures.

> Further action e.g. capability [procedures] might follow in time if appropriate. New objectives and closer monitoring may occur.

Several mentioned that they would not expect failure to meet an objective to come as a surprise to them as they should already have been aware if a teacher was having serious problems. Some heads, however, expressed their own, or their colleagues' bewilderment at such an outcome:

This is never a surprise, as we have review meetings once a term.

Generally this is a very contentious area that as a head I feel very uncertain of and am not confident in leading my team leaders through.

What was clear was some teachers were rather surprised to have a judgement that they had not met some aspects of objectives. They didn't expect evaluation to suggest [the standards were] 'not met'.

The predominant pattern which emerged was of amicable discussions between the teacher and the team leader to establish the reasons for failure, consideration of whether the objective was still appropriate, modification, if necessary, and more time being given. The subject of money, however, appeared to have rarely been raised.

Difficulties with implementation

Just over half, 53 per cent of heads, said that their school had encountered difficulties with the implementation of performance management. A range of difficulties was cited: lack of training for themselves, their team leaders and their teachers; some staff failing to give performance management sufficient priority; other initiatives and Ofsted inspections taking precedence; staff changes and illness; resistance in some schools to performance management and the threat of union action; and disruption to lessons caused by the need to cover team leaders.

The overwhelming difficulty once more, mentioned by over three-quarters of respondents, was the *time* that the performance management procedure required:

It's become a Frankenstein, soaking up all available time.

Finding the time to do the job properly. Not affording it time to develop the process. As one of the lowest funded schools in the country, finding time for such activities is challenging.

Fitting it all in time-wise, some funding for non-contact time would be useful.

Further analysis of the data indicated that primary schools have particular problems in allocating and funding the time needed. Non-contact time is less common in primary schools, so with their smaller staff it often means that the lessons of both the team leader and the teacher need to be covered. Not one secondary head reported problems in organising cover, but 10 per cent of primary heads in this sample did. It can be costly and difficult to secure quality supply teachers:

> It is often difficult to find time and supply cover to make it happen when planned.

> Time management – availability of good supply teachers, disruption to children's lessons.

Impact of performance management

The impact of performance-related pay in general and performance management in particular on teachers' practice and attitudes is a very important issue. Heads were asked to comment on how they perceived the staff felt about performance management. To some extent this could be seen as a test of their own competence in implementing the process, so it was no surprise that most believed it was viewed positively, although 70 per cent opted for *quite positive* compared with only 9 per cent who thought their staff viewed it *very positively*. Reasons given included: that teachers valued the allocation of quality time for professional dialogue about their performance and career ambitions, recognition of their strengths and achievements, systematic identification of their professional development needs and subsequent training and/or support provided.

Some heads also mentioned that they believed that their staff felt positive about the procedure because it was being 'well managed' and was seen as 'non-threatening' in their school, sometimes having been built upon existing successful appraisal procedures. Only a small number indicated that the prospect of more pay was a factor.

A few heads, particularly primary, indicated that, although the majority of their teachers had accepted the performance management procedure in a positive way, not all their staff had. A number of primary heads drew the distinction between older and younger members of their team:

> Younger staff (keen to move upwards) accept its value far more readily.

> Accepted by the majority as part of their professional development. The 'time-servers' see it as yet another imposition by management.

In the 14 per cent of schools where heads reported that teachers were reacting negatively to the procedure, the main reason seemed to be the additional workload it created, although a small number of heads reported that their staff disliked the link to pay.

Impact on classroom practice

One of the main reasons for introducing any policy or initiative in teaching is to exert a positive influence on classroom practice and then hopefully make a concomitant impact on pupil achievement. Table 6.6 shows what impact heads thought performance management was having on improving classroom practice.

There are many ways of interpreting these results. The data show that only 10 per cent felt performance management had made 'a lot' of impact, while just over half opted for the more muted 'some', and about a quarter said 'a little'. Only 6 per cent judged that it was having no impact. Some headteachers did offer a comment on this impact, a number qualifying their endorsement with reservations:

A lot:

> It relates directly to improving the quality of teaching and learning.

> Not always a positive impact though. Some staff perceive the focus on pupil performance as stressful and while that can contribute to improved outcomes it does not necessarily follow that the quality of teaching and learning are improving.

Some:

> Not as much as our school monitoring which is far more part of a 'whole' school approach to improvement.

> Performance management is the formal framework, if you will, for professional development and it combines with other strategies to improve classroom practice.

Table 6.6 What impact do you think performance management is having on improving classroom practice?

Impact on practice	Percentage
A lot	10
Some	53
A little	27
None	6
Don't know	1
Mixed	2

Note: These figures do not total 100 due to rounding.

It is the shared focus that performance management has helped to bring about, along with the more open sharing of classroom practice between colleagues.

A little:

Not a lot really – happens anyway, without performance management.

None

Classroom improvement is not made by this system.

Teachers have always self-evaluated and are professional in their approach. As headteacher I support and develop their self-evaluation skills. Far more important for improving teaching!

The implementation of performance related pay

Over 97 per cent of the headteachers sampled had teachers who had gone through the pay threshold and were eligible to be considered for an increment on the upper pay scale. Those heads were asked what criteria their school would use to decide whether a teacher would be granted a further increment on this upper pay scale. The prospect had sent many heads turning to their professional association or fellow heads. Nearly two-thirds (62 per cent) said they had been in contact with their union, while 52 per cent had discussed it formally within their local consortium of headteachers, and 58 per cent informally with other local heads. Although local education authorities were not required to become involved directly in the performance management procedure, 63 per cent of heads had contacted their LEA about what criteria should be applied and 18 per cent had contacted the DfES. The most common reason given for consulting others was uncertainty and lack of sufficient guidance:

No clear guidance from anyone. National criteria should have been set rather than asking individual schools to keep reinventing the wheel. Application form needed [for people seeking to progress to higher points].

No clear advice. ANYWHERE!!

I think we should have been given a clear lead and set of criteria by DfES. There is still a *lot* of uncertainty and confusion amongst heads.

By contrast, one head favoured autonomy over too much guidance:

I do not agree with colleagues who want a standard form. Each school context is slightly different. We need the freedom to implement our own scheme.

Schools are responsible for their own budgets and salaries can absorb three-quarters or more of the money available, especially in small schools. The issue of funding pay increases was a particularly important one for heads. It was also very worrying for the 41 per cent of heads who did not think they would have adequate funds, but knew they would need to find money to pay the successful, usually taking it from elsewhere:

> This will cause enormous problems for the school, which will inevitably have a deficit budget.

> No, we will not have sufficient from the grant (who will?). We will make up the difference from our delegated budget – less money for the pupils yet again ...

> We do have the funds, but it means we will not spend this money on the pupils.

> Okay because we have cut back on other areas/resources/redecoration/ support staff.

What criteria would be used to determine who would receive an additional increment was another issue. Heads' comments showed that, providing teachers had maintained their threshold standards, they were meeting the 'substantial and sustained' type of performance described in the official pay and conditions document, and would therefore receive an increment:

> 'Substantial' and 'sustained' are the *only* criteria.

> Sustained performance since threshold. We've put in the pay policy 'substantial and sustained' but in practice we want them to have maintained performance since threshold.

> Criteria suggested by the unions. We have been unable to implement any other criteria due to timescale. Unions are quite clear that we are unable to put other criteria in place. I had wanted to implement my own set, but I couldn't go ahead.

Some heads still wanted further information and stated that they would also consider whether teachers had met their performance management objectives. A few were also considering additional information such as a teacher's contribution to the school, or on occasion the information gathered from lesson observations or an Ofsted visit:

1. Progress towards objectives – reported back from performance management reviews.

2. Scrutiny of performance data and other relevant issues that might have a bearing on whether they are still meeting all threshold criteria.

Observation evidence and ... performance management reviews plus other evidence the teacher may wish to share at a meeting I organise with them.

Modifications to the procedures

Nearly a third of respondents said they would modify their performance management procedures in the light of experience. A number used the word *sustained*, to indicate that they were looking for evidence that improvements and modifications had persisted beyond the immediate appraisal process. The most common features mentioned were ensuring that objectives were more challenging, more specific or more closely matched to the school's development plan or to national standards:

Tighter description of more challenging targets.

Objectives need to be more specific and measurable – too vague in past.

There will need to be more rigour, rather than the 'feel good' factor.

Only a few said that they would make greater use of measurements of pupil progress, or look for evidence of impact on pupil learning or teaching quality.

Advantages of performance management

Headteachers were asked what they saw as the advantages, if any, of the government's performance management procedure. A fifth of primary heads and a quarter of secondary heads in the sample said 'None', but the remainder were more positive. The procedure was welcomed for being 'statutory' and for providing 'a systematic framework'. Some heads indicated that an effective process for monitoring had already been in place in their school but felt the introduction of the statutory procedure would ensure that all schools addressed this issue.

The inclusion of the formal Review meeting at which teacher and team leader have time allocated to discuss past performance, professional development needs, career ambitions and the teacher's role within the wider School Development/School Improvement Plan was particularly welcomed. A majority of heads believed that focusing on teachers' performance, celebrating strengths, sharing good practice, interrogating pupil progress data and setting annual objectives would ultimately result in improvements in teaching and learning in their schools:

> It emphasises very strongly the teacher's professional commitment. The philosophy fits in well with current thinking in relation to the self-evaluating, self-improving school. It places the emphasis very strongly on teaching and learning.

> It assists with focus on school development. It encourages sharing of good practice. It ensures teachers receive support. If it can lead to increased pay, it adds incentives.

There was, however, little explicit enthusiasm for the link to pay. Only 20 per cent of primary heads and 14 per cent of secondary heads responding to this question mentioned benefits associated with linking teachers' pay and performance, but those who did said they valued the opportunity to reward their good teachers financially and a small number believed it would aid retention and recruitment in the profession.

Disadvantages of performance management

Headteachers were fulsome in their description of the *disadvantages* of the government's performance management procedure. Although some of the most scathing comments were made by those who said they were unable to identify any *advantages* to the system, many heads who had made positive comments also listed a number of disadvantages. Overwhelmingly, the head-teachers were critical of the amount of time the procedure consumes, the amount of bureaucracy it created, the additional workload it placed on senior and middle managers, and the lack of funding for the process in general. This last point was made particularly strongly by primary headteachers who needed to buy in supply cover to enable teachers and team leaders to meet, due to the lack of non-contact time in primary schools.

Some heads felt that the procedure had been too hastily introduced by the government and also disliked the imposition of what they saw as a 'one size fits all' process which ignored the uniqueness of schools. The potential divisiveness of the procedure was commented on and a number felt that, rather than improve teachers' morale, it could disillusion and demotivate, if teachers who felt they should receive pay increments were not awarded them:

> Not thought out before implementation. Not valued by staff. Does not generate a 'team' effort. Yet more paper to process.

I feel the whole thing has been badly handled and put heads at odds with their staff. Seen as a further centralised initiative and an additional burden. Too little time to be done effectively. Relating pay to performance review removes any incentive to admit and remedy weaknesses. Headteacher stress!

Headteachers also reiterated their frustration at the lack of clarity from the government about the criteria to be applied when judging whether teachers should progress further up the upper pay spine. A myriad of other disadvantages were mentioned: the lack of consistency in implementation between schools; the emphasis on pupil performance data which might not be reliable; the disruption caused to lessons when team leaders and teachers had to meet; the potential lack of objectivity by team leaders; and the problems faced by schools from union opposition to the procedure, but each of these disadvantages was only mentioned by a small number of heads. It was clear from the data that the overriding concerns of heads are 'time', 'bureaucracy' and 'the lack of funding'. The quotations below illustrate the variety of headteachers' responses to performance management:

Generally, I welcome [performance management] and will use it as a tool to promote further improvements in results. My caution over the divisive nature and the threat to goodwill remains. However, I will endeavour to operate it in such a way that it is viewed positively and delivered humanely – it is in my power to influence that.

I believe it is a tragedy for the profession (as I have seen the first elements of internal divisiveness in the staff room on matters of pay I remember witnessing in my career.) It represents a significant erosion of professional good will which will probably never be regained.

It wastes time, adds pressure. The idea is good but our system is very informal and I do not feel capable of judging my staff. That's not how I work. It is hateful. I do enjoy sitting and discussing objectives for this year. It is fraught with problems. It takes able teachers out of the classroom.

Factors influencing heads' judgements

Headteachers' responses were analysed separately for different groups. Two particular types of comparison were of special interest:

* length of service – possible differences between more and less experienced heads;
* age range of school – possible differences between primary and secondary heads.

Length of service

The sample was very evenly distributed across five categories of length of service, covering: up to three years, 4–7 years, 8–11 years, 12–15 years, and 16+ years. The numbers of headteachers in each category ranged from 199 to 235. In general length of service was not a large discriminator and there were few aspects where it was significant, but over four matters there was a notable division according to length of experience. *Longer serving heads* (in the 12–15 and 16+ years of service categories), in contrast to their less experienced counterparts:

- were *more likely* to ask senior management to decide teachers' objectives (chi-square significant at the .02 level)
- were *less likely* to say they had problems with objective setting (chi-square significant at the .05 level)
- were *less likely* to have teachers who were thought to be unsuccessful at meeting their objectives (chi-square significant at the .001 level)
- were *less likely* to be in favour of linking pay with performance (chi-square significant at the .01 level).

These differences may be explained by a number of factors. Some new heads had clearly been brought in to act as a new broom, or to redeem a school that was not thought to be succeeding, so their attitudes might well be expected to be different. The experience divide on attitude to performance-related pay itself was especially notable. Among heads who had been in post under three years, some 56 per cent were in favour of linking pay to performance, while in the 12–15 and 16+ bracket it was only 29 per cent.

Primary and secondary heads

The split between primary and secondary heads in the sample was roughly in the proportion 60:40. There were several notable differences between these two sets of headteachers, including the ones below. *Primary heads*, in contrast to their secondary counterparts:

- were *more likely* to let some teachers decide their own objectives (chi-square significant at the .001 level)
- were *more likely* to say they were satisfied with the training they had received (chi-square significant at the .001 level)
- were *more likely* to say they had sufficient funds to pay teachers awarded a pay bonus (chi-square significant at the .01 level)
- were *less likely* to say they had problems with objective setting (chi-square significant at the .001 level)
- were *less likely* to use 'value added' measures of pupil progress, some 63 per cent doing so, compared with 73 per cent of secondary heads (chi-square significant at the .001 level)

- were *less likely* to have teachers who were thought to be unsuccessful at meeting their objectives, 45 per cent experiencing this compared with 70 per cent of secondary heads (chi-square significant at the .001 level)
- were *less likely* to be in favour of linking pay with performance, 36 per cent primary, 46 per cent secondary (chi-square significant at the .01 level).

The intimacy of the smaller size of primary schools probably explains some of these differences, but it is especially interesting to note some of the bigger gaps between the two groups. Secondary school heads, while still in the main opposed to performance-related pay, are more positive than their primary colleagues, possibly because the latter are very close to teachers, not usually shielded by senior and middle management, and so have to live directly and unavoidably with the consequences of decisions made.

In summary: are heads for or against performance-related pay?

Two years earlier we had asked a similar national sample of heads whether they were in favour of performance-related pay, as described in Chapter 3. At that time 60 per cent said they were opposed to it, compared with 39 per cent who said they were in favour. This position had barely changed, with 56 per cent of heads now saying they were not in favour. Supporters were divided in two, with about 29 per cent expressing no reservations and 11 per cent saying 'yes, but with reservations'. Three per cent were still unsure. Secondary heads were keener than primary, and newcomers were more in favour than longer serving heads.

Heads who said 'yes' unequivocally were strongly in favour of only rewarding *good* teachers and saw the statutory link between performance and pay as legitimising this action. Those who qualified their approval called for 'clear' and 'national' criteria on which to base their judgements about teachers' performance. They also wanted sufficient funding to be provided by the government to pay all those teachers deserving of an increment, rather than relying on schools to make up shortfalls.

The majority of heads who were firmly against linking teachers' performance and pay put forward a range of reasons. Some argued the process was based on a flawed theory of motivation and believed that performance-related pay had not proved successful in other fields. Others talked in terms of the consequences in terms of the additional workload and bureaucracy which this particular scheme had brought about for themselves and their senior and middle managers. Several heads still worried that the system would prove divisive, counter-productive to effective team-working.

What was especially notable, however, was that the figure of about 60 per cent of headteachers being opposed to performance-related pay, and 40 per cent being in favour, albeit sometimes with reservations, had remained remarkably and robustly consistent over the whole of the two-year period that separated our two national surveys.

7 Being managed

The teacher perspective

In the hierarchical pyramid structure under which a national education system operates, teachers who spend most of their time in their classroom are the bottom layer. The performance-related pay programme studied in this research project was introduced by the government. Its precepts then rippled down to headteachers via a private training agency employed by the government. Headteachers in turn had to induct teachers in their schools, even though they themselves, as was revealed in previous chapters, were often hostile to the idea, or sometimes vague about its associated procedures.

By the time a policy reaches classroom level it has passed through successive filters. Headteachers who are uncommitted to it may do the minimum necessary to ensure it is implemented. Others may use the process to firm and confirm their normal management style. At the end of this chain, teachers are faced with a dilemma. Irrespective of their own position on performance-related pay they either will, or will not be in receipt of more money if they are deemed to be 'performing' effectively.

In Chapter 4 we described how some teachers even took a stand and refused to submit themselves for consideration when invited, at the first stage of the process, *threshold assessment*, to apply to cross the pay threshold and become eligible for the higher salary scale. This chapter now moves ahead to the next phase of the performance-related pay procedure, relating teachers' reactions to and experiences of the whole operation of *performance management*, the general system for linking pay and performance that schools were expected to introduce.

In the neat diagrams and flow charts of policy as it appears on paper, there are usually no hurdles, obstacles or hitches as the process ripples down smoothly from policy-maker to practitioner. In actuality, however, implementation of a policy is usually uneven, variegated, and not always consonant with the wishes and aspirations of its begetters. It was precisely to document these craggy realities, and to see how performance-related pay policies worked out in practice, that we undertook intensive case studies of 32 teachers in twelve primary and secondary schools throughout the three-year period of the research. The teachers were interviewed at key stages of the process, as were their headteachers, and we also undertook observations of their lessons.

Where both the teacher and team leader agreed, we were present at each teacher's planning/review meetings. Any relevant documentation produced by the school was also collected.

Studying policy-into-process at classroom level allowed many research questions to be addressed. How did performance-related pay and performance management work out in practice? Was the implementation of the policy uniform or varied? What was the nature of relationships between key players, such as teachers and their team leaders, the people assigned to them to monitor their 'performance'? How were objectives set and monitored? Did teachers change for the better their teaching styles and classroom practices, what they actually did in their daily teaching? Who received and who did not receive an additional merit payment, and what was the reaction?

The 32 case study teachers worked in schools where the research team had interviewed the headteachers at the very beginning of the research project, to give continuity and to maximise the timespan covered. A range of different types of primary and secondary schools was selected and the teachers in them were given letters asking if they would like to volunteer to be studied during the period of the research. Replies were confidential, so headteachers did not know who had chosen to volunteer and who had not. Each of the 32 teachers was interviewed using semi-structured interview schedules at least twice. The initial interview took place towards the beginning of the first full school year of the project, the second a year later. Many teachers were interviewed three or even four times. Lesson observations took place not with a view to tracking changes, but rather to give the flavour of the teacher's life in the classroom as a background to other forms of data collection.

The nature and amount of contact with case study teachers varied for a number of reasons. We did not want to influence events by giving the impression that we wished teachers to progress their performance management procedure any faster than would have been the case had we not been monitoring it. If some teachers had not had their review meeting when our interviews were planned, for example, we simply returned later. Some teachers had also agreed that we could watch their lessons, so they were interviewed additionally before and after the lesson observation.

In certain cases, as is often the case in a longitudinal study such as this, there was 'sample mortality', a sinister sounding term which only means that some teachers moved schools during the period of the research or for other reasons were unable to continue their participation. Two teachers were promoted to deputy headships, and became subject to a different performance management regime; one left teaching; a fourth changed school. The final sample on whom we had the full picture, therefore, was twenty-eight. At the end of the project, three years later, we undertook a final and lengthy interview with sixteen of the teachers in eight schools. This chapter describes and analyses the main themes emerging from these case studies. In Chapter 8, five contrasting case studies will be discussed, to illustrate the personal detail of what the performance management process had involved for individual teachers.

Teachers' initial opinions of performance management

When we interviewed the 32 teachers towards the beginning of the research, three linked questions were asked to investigate their views of the process at that time: What do you think are the aims of performance management? What do you think are the advantages, if any? What do you think are the disadvantages, if any?

The majority of teachers said that they believed that the government's intention was to raise teaching standards. Some felt the government hoped to achieve this by 'ensuring that teachers are doing their job properly', others by 'encouraging poor teachers to leave the profession', and occasionally it was seen as 'yet another form of inspection'. Only a quarter at this early stage mentioned the link to pay. These were divided as to the government's motive in this respect between those who felt the government was trying to increase the levels of pay within the profession to aid recruitment and retention and those who felt that it was 'a tool for giving us a harder time'.

When asked what they saw as the advantages of the procedure, it was clear that most teachers believed that, if implemented properly, it should indeed bring about improvements in performance. Some talked of the benefits of having a clear structure within which to appraise practice:

> I think the advantages will be that perhaps our aims and objectives will be clearer. I think the government's aim is to improve standards and ours is too. There are a lot of benefits. I think performance management is good.

Others referred to particular aspects of the procedure which they saw as beneficial to their own professional development: the opportunity for self-reflection, recognition of their strengths and achievements, discussion of their career aspirations, the sharing of good practice, and the identification of any support or training which might be useful:

> I hope I'll gain recognition of my achievements. And that I'll get some helpful criticism which will help me to improve my performance. That's not always been available in the past. People are sometimes diffident about telling you.

> In the past, because I'm a line manager, people assume that I can do it all. My own professional development needs have not been so well addressed. I'm hoping for more professional development opportunities.

Although the link with pay was not at the forefront of most teachers' minds in initial interviews, some did specifically state that they hoped to get more money, occasionally expressing concern about the conflict between honesty and securing cash rewards:

> Money. To be honest, very little else, because for me it won't do anything I don't already do and that doesn't exist here.

> At the moment performance management is there purely as an academic process, so one can be as honest as one wants, and seek help. But if it's linked to pay, I would disguise my weaknesses and enhance my strengths in order to get the money ... At the moment I can be honest and seek help. If it's linked to fifteen hundred pounds in my pocket – no way – I'll show where I'm good.

Others felt they would gain nothing from the performance management procedure but more pressure:

> Personally nothing, except more paperwork.

> Nothing ... [laughs] ... A nervous breakdown? It's just too much stress, there's just too much pressure nowadays.

While nearly all teachers could find *something* positive in the procedure, there were still many concerns about how it would work in practice. Five major disadvantages were predicted: (1) the additional stress/pressure it would cause, (2) the amount of bureaucracy generated, (3) the time it would take, (4) its potential divisiveness, and (5) problems with measuring pupil progress. A small number of teachers mentioned additional disadvantages: the pressures of being observed, and the potential slump in morale if schools concentrated only on teachers' weaknesses, ignoring their strengths.

Training

Each of the teachers studied had received some sort of training for performance management. In most cases, a whole day had been devoted to it, sometimes combined with the first planning meetings, but two schools had used twilight sessions. The quality of the training varied from school to school. One secondary school tried to make the training session a worthwhile experience for staff by involving both its own senior managers and external advisors in running it, but the day had not been a success:

> Many felt it was appalling. There was a lack of co-ordination. All of them told us different things. It reaffirms my view that no-one knows what they're doing.

In contrast, the head of another secondary school had personally led an in-service training day which had included seminar groups discussing in detail the qualities of effective teachers and the issues surrounding target setting. The teachers at this school were positive about their training, as the comment below shows:

> It was good ... [I feel] very well informed now. I also have lots of documents provided by the school to refer to.

Inevitably, there were some schools where teachers differed in their views of the training they had received. The majority, however, stated that they felt reasonably well informed about the process before they embarked upon it.

Team leaders

A crucial element, if performance management is to be effective, is the relationship between teacher and team leader. We were interested to examine the nature of these relationships to investigate whether linking pay to performance would influence the way in which such relationships functioned. Factors like mutual trust and respect were shown in one of our earlier studies of teacher appraisal (Wragg *et al.* 1996) to be important, influencing how frank people would be about their perceived weaknesses and the extent to which they might change their behaviour and strategies.

With interviewees who were themselves team leaders of other teachers, we concentrated solely on their relationship with and views of their own team leaders. Most team leaders in secondary schools were line managers: usually heads of the teacher's department or age phase. Secondary teachers who were relatively senior themselves were often supervised by their deputy head. In primary schools, the structure is flatter, so a teacher's team leader was often the head. In schools with a large senior management team, the teachers did not usually know who had made the final decision about who their team leader would be, though in one case it had been left to the deputy head and in another it had been decided within the departments. Many teachers said that they were 'just told' who their team leader would be and several said the selection was 'automatic' because one person was the obvious choice.

Most teachers were happy with their team leader, even though few had been involved in the selection. Common descriptors were 'fine', 'happy', or that it was 'fair enough', while some were more positively enthusiastic. Only a small number were not happy:

> It's nothing personal, but she wouldn't have been the person I would have chosen, but I didn't feel strongly enough to go and say 'Oh no, not her'. But she's not the person I would have chosen myself.

> I was just told. I didn't like it but I thought I ought to give it a go first.

All the dissatisfied teachers were in secondary schools. Heads of departments in particular did not like being appraised by an equal ranking colleague from a different discipline. The main reason for their dissatisfaction seemed to be more lack of the relevant subject and pedagogical knowledge, rather than a status or personality clash. Team leaders who taught a different subject were thought to be unable to appreciate the particular difficulties or characteristics of the teacher's own discipline:

> I would rather have had someone who was not a history teacher. I would have preferred someone who understands how English works.

> He's a scientist. He thinks differently.

When performance management was being introduced, teachers were asked, in the initial interview, what they saw as the role of the team leader. They usually highlighted the help and advice they expected to get. Some saw the role in *broad* terms, expecting a facilitator who would 'enable people to improve, see what they're good at and address their weaknesses', 'share good practice' or 'develop teachers' efficacy for the benefit of students'. Others expected *specific* help: to set 'realistic' or 'personally significant' targets and then to give support to achieve them with guidance and feedback. Although teachers had many reservations about various aspects of the actual process in these initial interviews, the relationship with and the role of their team leader was not generally stated to be a cause of anxiety.

When the forerunner to performance management, teacher appraisal, had been introduced into schools by the UK government in 1992, team leaders were at that time known as 'appraisers'. They had talked about the need to make the process *beneficial* for their 'appraisees' and some had felt insecure about their position, wondering if they could offer very much in the way of advice to their colleagues (Wragg *et al.* 1996). Interviews undertaken with performance management team leaders in the present study, nearly a decade later, revealed a harder approach, more overtly focused on reaching targets and rectifying perceived weaknesses. This was not too surprising, given the cultural shift in attitude towards greater accountability during the intervening years:

> My role is to monitor, help set objectives, see if they're fulfilled.

> My role is not to impose a target. With my knowledge of that person, it's to tease out ways for them and their work, even if they don't agree.

> I perceive myself as an encourager, to point out weaknesses in performance, to enhance the performance of the department. A by-product is their own professional development. The department is more important.

In most cases the pairing of teacher and team leader remained the same over the full three years of this study and in all but one case the relationship was described in positive terms by the teacher. In the majority of cases, the relationship between teacher and team leader was collegial rather than superior-subordinate. The tone in review meetings was predominantly one of negotiation and compromise, although there were two cases where tensions occurred during discussions to set the teachers' objectives. In one of these, described in detail in Chapter 8, the team leader imposed objectives, but later modified them in response to the teacher's concerns. In the second, a head of department in a large secondary felt that his own personal development had been inhibited by his team leader's almost exclusive focus on examination results:

> I have to say my review meeting was tacked onto the end of the departmental exam results review meeting so we had like an hour, an hour and a bit, of which the exam results lasted for about three-quarters of an hour, so the review of my other objectives, we're talking fifteen minutes here ... It's not aided my own critical review of where I'm going.

Implementation

The original Model Performance Management Policy produced by the Department for Education and Employment (DfEE) had specified that, for teaching staff, 'in the first cycle, the first meeting and setting of objectives should have taken place ... before the end of February 2001' (DfEE 2000a: 2, para 5). In seven of the 12 case study schools, the planning meeting had indeed taken place by this deadline, but in the other five slippage had occurred. In one school, the head appeared uncommitted to the process and left at the end of the year, so the procedure took even longer. Slippage was least common when the school had allocated an in-service day for meetings and most frequent when arrangements were left to the team leader and teacher.

When interviewed a year later, teachers were polarised, a large majority perceiving their own performance management procedure either to be going well or to be making little impact. These two categories were not always mutually exclusive, because for some teachers hostile to performance-related pay, the whole process having little impact was regarded as a good thing. Praise from those who thought it was going well was muted, expressed in language, like 'sensible', and 'OK – an interesting process'. Some of those who felt the 'new' procedures were making little impact explained that this was because most of the elements were not new at all, but were part of their normal routine. The process was described as 'things I would have done anyway', and meetings were 'part of a dialogue I would expect to have with those I work with'.

While two-thirds of the sample were happy or relatively satisfied with the implementation in their school generally, *very* enthusiastic comments were rare and the line between those rated as 'positive' and merely 'accepting' was a thin one – the line between 'OK, it doesn't worry me' and 'painless'. Approximately one-third were decidedly disgruntled. Common terms used were 'ineffective', 'patchy', 'low priority' and 'grossly inefficient', and they felt alienated, resigned or annoyed at its cursory and fragmented nature:

> I think of it as something that is done to me, not something I'm involved with.

> It has had no impact whatsoever. It's an abject waste of time, in general, for all teachers. Because it has no impact on what happens in the classroom.

> I don't feel it is going. I don't really think about it. I'm irritated it exists. I'm very self-motivated and I don't need things like this to make me work hard.

Where implementation worked well, the impetus almost always came from senior management, or the head alone. These heads allocated sufficient time for meetings and observations, distributed information, reminded teachers of deadlines, or arranged training for them:

> The head has kept on top of it and puts it in the school timetable so we know what's happening, and she gets on with it.

At the end of the project, when 16 of the original 32 teachers were interviewed intensively for a final time, it was immediately apparent that unevenness of implementation had been a significant feature throughout the whole process, confirming what we reported about headteachers' perceptions in Chapter 6. By the time half the teachers were into their third cycle, some had only just begun the second cycle, one had almost completed the first, while another described the process as having 'fizzled out'.

Setting objectives

In most schools the initial planning meeting eventually became combined with the review meeting to make one annual meeting, at which previous objectives were also discussed and judgements made as to whether they had been achieved. Government rules about setting objectives required teachers to devise ones that covered 'pupil progress, as well as ways of developing and improving teachers' professional practice', and were 'challenging [and] flexible' (DfEE 2000b: 6). Sources of evidence for pupil progress objectives were to include 'external and internal assessments, PANDAs [Performance and Assessment data] and benchmarking data' (DfEE 2000b: 14). Continuous attention to the teacher's progress during the year was envisaged as including 'short informal discussions and classroom observation' (DfEE 2000b: 7).

In practice our study revealed that most teachers agreed their objectives through discussion of their own ideas and preferences with their team leader, though in most cases these tended to be located within a framework identified by the school and at least one objective was usually related to the school development or school improvement plan. Only a few teachers said that they alone had decided their objectives. Irrespective of their genesis, almost all teachers expressed contentment with their objectives:

> They are sensible and practical. All things I would have done anyway.

> Yes. They're challenging and I was never expected to be 100 per cent successful with them.

By the end of the period of the research the majority of teachers' objectives contained at least one relating to pupil performance, by then a government requirement. In most schools the procedures hardly changed during the three years, but two teachers in different schools claimed they had detected a tightening in the approach, particularly in relation to the pupil performance objective:

> In our targets this year, we were asked to look at exam percentages. We weren't last year.

> We're now expected to have numerical targets relating to percentages for pupil progress.

In some schools very precise sounding targets were set, in terms of children's performance in national or standardised tests. In others, 'value added' calculations were undertaken:

> 50 per cent [of pupils are expected to get] A/A* at GCSE in my top ability set.

> We collect data from CATs [Cognitive Ability Tests], GCSEs, SATs [Standard Assessment Tests], AS/A2, and we make predictions on past performance. We do it after every set of exams for each department and individual teachers.

In one school where implementation had been erratic, not only did no teacher have a single pupil performance objective, but their responses to the question 'Are pupil performance data being gathered in relation to your performance management objectives?' revealed that they were not even aware that this was a requirement:

> Is that allowed? I don't think it is.

> Not in relation to personal objectives.

> Extremely unlikely. I wouldn't think my team leader knows anything about it.

Not one single case study teacher was unequivocally in favour of the use of pupil achievement data to assess teachers' performance. Even those generally in favour had reservations and critics displayed a particularly strong distrust of this kind of measure:

> It's fine as long as it's not the sole criterion used.

> It's fine when the results are good. But if they're bad, it's only one facet. It's not the only facet which should be used to judge performance.

> I'm not very happy. I don't think those collecting the data have enough experience of statistics to make reliable use of the data.

> I'm not happy about it. There are so many factors at work giving it a credence it doesn't possess. There are so many things affecting kids' performance. And it's not an exact science.

Despite many criticisms of and problems with using pupil performance data in this way (Goldstein 2001), as well as teachers' own reservations, both primary and secondary schools collected and processed a large amount of such data. The national headteacher questionnaire survey, discussed in Chapter 6, revealed that many schools not only made use of national test scores, they also undertook further optional tests at the end of each year. Many schools, particularly in the secondary sector, also used commercially produced 'value added' software packages to enable them to set targets for students.

Progress towards objectives

Interviews after the first year of implementation revealed general indifference among teachers, with little sense of ownership being expressed. As was the case in our study of teacher appraisal nearly a decade earlier, many teachers could not even remember their objectives when asked:

> I can't remember offhand, but I've got a note of them at home.

> I know I had to go on a course, and I had to review the rewards system. And I can't remember what the third one was. I think it was curriculum based, but it was something that we do anyway, or we would be doing anyway, I can't remember what it was specifically.

> One was about the library, and I think one was writing a literacy/media scheme and I've forgotten what the third one says. That shows how much they mean to me!

In most schools, as objectives were set, teachers had the opportunity to identify any support they might need in order to meet them. This usually took the form of extra training with some teachers having help within the school and some going on externally run courses. Other forms of support included being given lesson cover and one teacher was allocated money for additional classroom assistant help in processing pupil performance data. Not all teachers received support: sometimes because they had not felt they needed it, sometimes because it was not available.

When discussing difficulties encountered in meeting objectives, it was extremely rare for teachers to consider that their objectives had been too ambitious. The most frequently mentioned obstacle was time:

> Lack of time and energy – the objectives were clear, the time was given for the observation but then no other allocated times have really been set to actually sit down and work on the particular objective. Unfortunately, time is the most precious resource.

Less senior teachers sometimes expressed a feeling of impotence, being at the mercy of forces over which they had no control. While not specifically citing time, they often mentioned the constraint of 'other work' or 'greater priorities', in one case an Ofsted inspection. One teacher had been absent herself for five months, while the plans of several others had been disrupted by the absence or retirement of other members of staff. Resource issues were also mentioned: lack of appropriate computer equipment; lack of relevant courses or inability to attend appropriate courses, sometimes because the time or money was not provided:

> I wasn't allowed to go on a course. I was a bit miffed because my Head of Department went on hers, but I can't go on mine.

> I need an extensive one week course but I can't justify it and anyway I'd come back to chaos. That's just a fact of life with teaching. You can't afford time out of the classroom – you come back to piles of marking and equipment all over the place.

In the information sent to schools by the Department for Education and Employment when performance-related pay was first introduced, there was a requirement for 'continuous attention to the teacher's progress during the year' which was envisaged as including 'short informal discussions'. Only five teachers reported having meetings mid cycle to review progress and to discuss any support needed.

Lesson observations

Observation of classroom practice was one of the statutory elements of the performance management procedure. Two-thirds of the teachers interviewed at the very beginning of the process were unconcerned about being observed. For these, lesson observation had been an integral part of their school's monitoring procedures for some years, so they were used to it and found it a worthwhile experience:

> I'm always being observed. I've no worries about that.

> I feel fine about it. It's important. In your role as classroom teacher, it's important to be observed, and to observe others. It helps to share good practice.

> It's vital. Everyone should be observed all the time. It gets rid of nervousness, and helps build people up, if it's done properly, as it is here.

Some teachers, however, argued that lesson observations provide unreliable data because they are only a 'snapshot' of a teacher's classroom performance. Others simply felt nervous generally about being observed, though occasionally this was exacerbated by anxiety that a particular observation might be related to decisions about their salary:

> I feel very nervous because if the lesson doesn't go well, it could have a spiralling effect. If he then wanted to come and see another lesson, I would feel under such a strain.

> I find it hard to answer [how I feel about being observed as part of the performance management procedure] at the moment. It depends on who it is and what spirit it's being done in. One of the things that came up on our [training] day was that for it to work properly, teachers should feel they can focus on an area of difficulty, but no-one is going to do that when linked to pay or promotion. I'm going to want my best class to be seen.

In fact, little classroom observation was undertaken for performance management purposes in any of the case studies undertaken as part of this research. About half the teachers reported they had not been observed at all specifically for performance management purposes, though some had been observed as part of other school procedures, such as departmental reviews. About half had been observed once in each cycle. Observations were not usually related to the teacher's performance management objectives, but this was mainly because very few teachers had set objectives related to a specific aspect of their classroom practice, which in itself is a highly significant matter.

Review meetings

There was great variety in the structure and tone of review meetings. Most were businesslike, formal or semi-formal meetings, but some were little more than friendly informal conversations. One, which lasted only ten minutes, took place during morning break in the staffroom, with the teacher and team leader surrounded by other staff, who occasionally interrupted to clarify some administrative point with the team leader. The teacher later described it as 'nothing more than looking at the targets and giving them a tick or a cross'. However, the review meetings of the other two teachers studied in the same school had been formal, taking place in the team leader's office, during non-contact time for the teacher and had involved comprehensive discussion of the teacher's achievements over the cycle. These had lasted 50 minutes each – the full time allocated.

Only a quarter of teachers interviewed at the end of the project had met all their objectives. Most said they had met 'some'. One teacher had not had a review meeting at all, as her team leader had left, and so had reached her own decisions about whether she had achieved her objectives. In all other cases, the judgement as to whether objectives had been met was made by the teacher and team leader in discussion at the review meeting, although there were differences in how these decisions were reached. Some teachers were asked to provide documentary evidence, such as pupil performance data, or schemes of work. Others simply talked about how they had met their targets:

> I produced class performance data – pupil progress against national trends. And [the team leader checked] if I've produced something like a policy document; or evidence of using ICT in a lesson.

> [Judgements were made] by discussion with my team leader. I haven't had to give any evidence.

The discrepancies in the experiences of different teachers in the same school suggest that even where school managers believed that they had provided a systematic framework, it could be subverted by the action or inaction of individual team leaders and teachers, either deliberately, or simply because other priorities emerged.

Despite the different strategies adopted for deciding whether objectives had been met, between and within case study schools, most teachers expressed contentment with the methods used, though this was often because they were superficial and unthreatening:

> It's nice to get a bit of praise.

> I'm happy because it was easy, but I feel dissatisfied because it wasn't very thorough.

> I'm happy. I'd have been less happy if I'd had to spend hours and hours producing evidence.

A small number of teachers expressed negative feelings because they were unhappy with the meeting's outcomes. In certain cases this was because they felt coerced into agreeing new objectives they did not want, while others were dissatisfied because they could see no prospect of being able to achieve their targets:

> I felt that, although the targets were set, there was still no further information on how the targets were to be reached and no indication of extra support or actual timetabled non-contact time to fulfil the targets.

> The whole thing is a total waste of time because there's no support for the targets. They say time will be allocated for you to do things, but it just isn't.

Where teachers had failed to meet objectives, these were either carried over to the next cycle or, if they were perceived with hindsight to have been inappropriate, dropped altogether. There was no evidence of punitive action being taken by any school in this context, nor any example of a teacher in our sample failing to be awarded the next increment on the upper pay scale, even though a number had not met all their performance management objectives.

Impact on classroom practice

When the government first introduced performance management, it was in the expectation that it would raise standards of teaching. Eleven of the 32 case study teachers interviewed at the very beginning of the project predicted that it would have *no* impact on their practice, while three believed it would have a *negative* effect, blaming disruption to their normal working life and a narrowing of perspective due to specified objectives. Teachers saying it would have *no* impact defended this stance by insisting that they were already good teachers who reflect constantly on their practice, or that they were too old to change:

> I think I'm a good teacher and I do a good job. I think my students learn well, achieve their potential and enjoy my lessons. I don't honestly think I can improve on what I do. Perhaps at the beginning of my career it would have had an impact, but now I feel confident that I'm an effective teacher.

> It's too late for that. I've got three years till retirement. My overall style of teaching is unlikely to change.

Just over half believed that it would improve their classroom practice. Even this figure is deceptively high, because responses in interview often describe improvements in mood or morale, or access to courses, rather than changed teaching strategies. They identified several contributory factors: the sharper focus it would bring to their work, setting and meeting objectives, the constructive comments and suggestions for improvement which they hoped would be offered by their team leader, and being able to address their professional development needs, though there was sometimes scepticism about whether their aspirations would be met:

> Yes, because of the objectives that will be set and because the observation and feedback should show me ways of improving my practice.

> Yes, I'm hoping it will. If I don't meet my targets, then I'll expect to get training. I don't expect to meet one of my [classroom] targets. I actually manipulated that for my own purposes so that I can get the training.

> It may [affect my classroom practice], but I'm dubious about it. It may give me pointers to things I could do better. But it's highly dependent on the quality of the observation and I have reservations about the quality of feedback I might get.

The eventual outcome was a classic example of self-fulfilling prophesy. Nothing happened during the first year of performance management to make teachers change their minds. Those who originally believed the process would have no impact on their classroom practice reported, a year or so later, that it had not changed anything, for the reasons they had originally stated:

> No. Because there was nothing wrong with my classroom practice!

> No, there's nothing extra it has brought to me, because I do my job the best I can anyway.

> I just ignore it. I've tried to think about it, but I just carry on doing what I do.

The teachers who said that the process *had* made a difference to their classroom practice were mostly those who had originally expected this to happen. A few suggested that the greatest benefit came from the opportunity to have in-depth discussions with senior colleagues, while one mentioned being observed and another said it was observing others. For the majority, however, the outcome did not appear to be a radical modification of their teaching styles and strategies, more a slight change in their outlook or in the way they approached their job, or kept records of pupil progress. Some spoke of 'raised awareness', of being 'more reflective', and of 'focusing my mind'. One, more prosaically, said:

> It's made me log a lot more things about what I'm doing, even if I don't think they're particularly related to my objectives. So I've started a new portfolio just for this year.

Even when pressed, only two teachers were able to detail specific changes made to their classroom practice, like the one who, after being observed, said:

> The head sat down one day with a class map and noted who I discussed questions with and it was predominately people on the right-hand side of my body. I'd never realised that. That was quite a useful thing, so now I don't just point with my right hand, but I point with my left. So that's one very trivial point, but significant as well.

Another teacher of 16-year-old public examination candidates spoke of analysing pupil progress data with more care and then focusing on a group of pupils who were predicted a grade D or E in their exam. Since pupils need to obtain a grade C or better to count in published league table statistics, this technique of 'borderlining', i.e. boosting scores at the qualifying margins, is a commonly used tactic for improving examination results in schools. One teacher pointed out the difficulty of attributing any changes specifically to the performance management procedure:

> I don't know whether that's something I would have done anyway. It's funny how, when things become practice in a school anyway … it's very difficult to know what it was like before.

By the end of the three years the majority of teachers said that performance management had made no impact on their classroom practice, many stating that they were 'reflective teachers' who continually evaluate their own practice, or that the objectives would have been addressed anyway:

> You evolve as a teacher anyway. Once you stop evolving you should give up. I would have picked up new ideas anyway.

> The targets are so embedded in what the school does anyway. I do use ICT more as a classroom tool but I would have done anyway. All staff have been given a laptop and ICT training. It made sense to choose the targets I did because they were linked to the school development plan.

One teacher said that performance management should have brought about changes in her practice but the support that she had been promised had not been forthcoming. Another teacher dismissed the link to pay as a motivator for improving performance:

I haven't had performance-related pay in the past, but I've always tried to improve, for example, my ICT skills and I read a lot around my subject area and I attend meetings and I observe other teachers' lessons. Doing it for money is not a motivator. The incentive is to do your job well.

In cases where teachers reported that they had changed their practice, the credit was assigned mainly to the objective setting process, which had helped focus teachers' minds on a particular aspect of their performance, as well as to the suggestions made by the team leader following the lesson observation:

When he observed my lesson he suggested a few things which I took on board. By declaring my weaknesses, it made me more aware of it. I think I am now better at dealing with [this area of my classroom practice].

The findings throughout the three year period, confirmed by our own lesson observations, suggest that few teachers made significant changes to well-established classroom routines as a result of performance management. There appeared to be a variety of reasons for this, including the absence of classroom-related targets for most of the teachers in our sample, the teacher's own attitude towards the need for change and, in secondary schools, a disinclination to value feedback given by a team leader who worked within a different subject area.

These findings once again strongly echoed the results of research we conducted into the forerunner of performance management, teacher appraisal, in the 1990s. The conclusion reached then was that the strongest claim being made for that particular process was of 'greater awareness', and that 'revolutionary changes in classroom practice did not occur' (Wragg *et al.* 1996: 183).

The head described above, who focused the teacher on how questions were being distributed around the class, is one of the few cases encountered of teacher and team leader reflecting on and successfully reconceiving a specific interactive teaching and learning process. If such transactions are rare, it is difficult to see how there can be much modification of deeply ingrained teaching habits, either through the teacher appraisal procedures of the 1990s, or performance-related pay, unless a sharper and more explicit focus is given to changing behaviour for the better. These are matters we shall take up again in Chapter 9.

Performance management as a part of school management

As a general rule, performance management closely mirrored overall school management. Where this was irresolute or unintrusive, performance management itself often made little impact on staff:

It really hasn't made that much of an impact on me. It's very much in the distance. I think it's departmental. It depends on the strength of the department. My department is more relaxed.

It's a farce. I have no faith in it at all. If I can make up things and it's okayed, then it's not worth the paper it's written on.

While policy had failed to be implemented effectively at the macro level within this particular school, at classroom level certain individual teachers had nonetheless been determined to make a success of the procedure:

It's gone very well. It's allowed me to name and do specific things.

In those schools where overall management was well structured and effective, teachers were usually more likely to value the procedure:

It's been professional, well managed appraisal, rather than just a talking shop. That's good.

The structure is good and supportive.

There's been a clear structure. It's been very successful and rewarding. We're well informed here by senior management, in general.

This positive reaction to structured forms of management was not witnessed in every school we studied. In one school, where review meetings were organised on in-service days to ensure the procedure was implemented right across the school, one teacher still reported it to be a 'waste of time', while another talked of a 'lack of trust', and two indicated that performance management only entered their thinking the day before the annual review meeting. Teachers in this school talked of 'going through the motions'. Simply being well organised did not necessarily win the support of teachers subject to performance management, especially if there was lack of trust.

When teachers were asked once more to think about the advantages and disadvantages of the performance management procedure in our final interviews at the end of the research, a number said, 'For me, personally none, but ...' and then went on to identify benefits. These included the identification of areas of weakness which had led to improvements in performance, usually in relation to other colleagues rather than themselves; the way in which the objective setting process had made them focus on particular areas of their practice; the acknowledgement of their professional development needs; and the recognition of their achievements. Team leaders had found it to be an effective management tool, offering quality discussion time with colleagues and the opportunity to set common departmental objectives.

Some of the disadvantages predicted by teachers at the beginning of the process were not featured in the reactions at the end. The greatest lack of congruity was on the matter of *divisiveness*. There was no evidence that the procedure had proved particularly divisive, because almost all teachers had been rewarded with additional cash payments. It was more likely that anxieties relating to workload and bureaucracy had been realised. The link between performance and pay continued to be criticised by some teachers and in this context it was claimed by two teachers that there had been a shift in their team leader's role from that of supporter and facilitator to that of judge. An element initially unforeseen by teachers, and causing some unease, was the inconsistency in the way in which the procedure was implemented by different departments or different individuals within a school, and there were a few accusations of insufficient rigour.

When asked their expectations for the future, there was a strong consensus that the link between performance and pay would become stronger and an expectation that the procedure would become consequently more rigorous. Several teachers, nonetheless, either thought or hoped that it would eventually disappear.

Headteachers of the case study schools were positive about the procedure as a staff development tool. Teachers were felt to be benefiting from the objectives setting process by becoming more focused in their practice. There was, however, a notable lack of congruence in some schools between the head's and the teachers' perceptions of the process. Several heads argued that the imposition of a *statutory* procedure was unnecessary, because systematic monitoring and assessment had been taking place in their school for many years, yet interviews with teachers revealed that some schools studied in this research had previously undertaken little or no systematic monitoring.

Awarding merit payments

Those teachers who 'crossed the threshold' gained access to a higher salary scale and became eligible to receive a further merit award two years later, known within the profession as upper pay spine 2 (UPS2). During the course of our interviews with the headteachers of case study schools at the time these decisions had to be made, we asked them how they were going to decide which eligible teachers should receive the first increment on this upper pay scale.

Frustration was felt by heads over a number of matters. One common complaint was that the government was offering to fund no more than 80 per cent of the costs, while another was the lack of clear criteria on which the decisions should be made:

> I think the government has come unstuck on this – it's awful. We had external assessors for threshold assessment; they were not necessary – heads could do it. Now suddenly for the government to give 80 per cent of the funding required and to say 'it's up to headteachers' is a bit much!

The problem is the DfES haven't told me how much I'm going to get! It's crazy, isn't it? They say 'Implement the scheme, pay everyone from 1st September, but we're not going to tell you how much money you've got, and we're not going to give you nationally agreed criteria to use – but can you do it anyway, please'!

Of the twelve heads interviewed in case study schools, only three anticipated that *all* eligible staff would progress up the upper pay scale. One primary head said that current staff were 'excellent and deserve it', but did not believe that all eligible teachers nationally should be successful. In other cases, the heads cited recent inspections and said that, as the outcome had been so positive, they could not inform any members of staff that they were not worthy of the increment.

In the event heads felt they simply had to improvise their own criteria. In one school, team leaders were required to complete a form to indicate whether:

(a) the teacher had maintained all the threshold standards in a fully satisfactory manner; (b) the teacher had addressed any areas for further development identified either at threshold assessment or at performance review; and (c) the teacher had achieved or made good progress towards objectives agreed or set ... for the relevant period.

Two teachers in this school described this process as follows:

As a middle manager I had a form to fill in for colleagues – it took three or four minutes each. I had to sign my own form!

It was based on previous performance management targets. It wasn't really nitty-gritty. I didn't have to prove it. It was more about 'making progress' towards targets. I didn't have to apply. There were school forms [for applying to move up the higher scale], but they were for managers to complete. I got a letter saying I'd got it. But not everyone did.

In other schools teachers had no idea how decisions had been made, but believed all eligible teachers had received the additional increment. Of the teachers who were still waiting to hear whether they would be offered an award, almost all believed they would definitely receive it. Some teachers, however, were unhappy about the lack of discrimination, firmly believing that not everyone should be awarded the increment:

I'm not sure, within the time constraints, whether sufficient information is gathered to make decisions. I can see people who aren't so good getting the same as those rushing around. Are we rewarding *good* teachers? It devalues it if some can get it without working as much or as hard.

In one school where staff had been kept fully informed by the head of the criteria being applied, the teachers professed themselves as happy with the way in which it had been implemented. Unsurprisingly, there was much less satisfaction in schools where information had been sparse, particularly as those who should have been involved with the decision-making process were apparently excluded:

> I was unhappy at not knowing the procedure. I had to keep asking 'when?'. No-one could answer questions about what would happen and when.

> I would like to have had input, as head of department, for my own people. I wasn't consulted. I don't know how the decisions were made.

Conclusion

The teachers we studied began the process with a number of anxieties about pay being linked to performance. One of the most notable, that selecting some people for monetary rewards would be divisive, never materialised. Almost all teachers nationally passed through the pay threshold and then progressed up the higher salary scale, and the case study teachers mirrored this high degree of success. In the end the policy had become a general pay rise, rather than a searing scrutiny that divided schools and the profession.

Nor were certain other anxieties fulfilled. The relationship between teacher and team leader turned out to be unproblematic in most cases. Although teachers had usually played no role in the selection of their team leader, they were generally happy with the person chosen. Problems were most likely to occur when the team leader had a different teaching style, was not knowledgeable or experienced enough to guide professional development, or in secondary schools, when the team leader taught a different subject.

The agreement of objectives was not seen as a problem, as in most cases objectives had been agreed through discussion of teachers' own ideas and preferences, usually within a framework provided by the school. Setting objectives did not necessarily, however, propel teachers in new directions, since many said the objectives merely consisted of steps they would have taken anyway, with few feeling pushed into agreeing objectives they did not want. There was evidence that objectives were seen as not being especially exacting and some teachers obtained their salary bonus despite not having met all of them. Obstacles to achieving objectives included lack of time, other priorities, their own or someone else's absence, and lack of promised training.

There was considerable variation in the implementation of performance management, which tended to mirror the style of management already extant in the school. Under a laissez-faire regime responsibility for the procedure was usually left to individual pairings of teacher and team leader. Schedules were likely to slip as other priorities took over. More structured management ensured keeping to a timetable, though it did not guarantee commitment from participants, especially when there was lack of trust.

Nearly two-thirds of teachers had no concerns about being observed teaching. Most of these stated that lesson observation had been an integral part of their school's monitoring procedures for some years and they found it a worthwhile experience. A few questioned the reliability of observation evidence, either because it provided only a snapshot of their teaching or because they distrusted the person carrying out the observation. In reality, however, few lesson observations were carried out purely for the performance management procedure, rather than for other purposes.

There was little evidence of objectives being set that were specifically related to classroom practice. This may explain why teachers were likely to report being more reflective and focused, rather than making any significant changes to how they actually taught in their lessons. Some thought this was because they were already good teachers who did the best they could, or that they were too old to change. Several could not even remember what their objectives were, when asked.

In schools where systematic monitoring of teachers' performance had been in place for some years already, teachers were much less anxious about the introduction of performance management. Where monitoring had previously been infrequent, or where teachers had judged the amount to be low, the procedure took longer to become embedded. The wide variation in implementation meant that teachers had vastly different experiences of the procedure. For some it never became a significant feature. Even for those in schools where it was taken more seriously, it only became a priority for many as the time approached for their annual meeting with their team leader. In order to give more of the flavour of what the process meant for the teachers involved in it, we shall describe five case study teachers in greater detail in Chapter 8.

8 Performance-related pay in action

Five case studies

Performance-related pay was a policy which was imposed on 24,000 primary and secondary schools rather than introduced by the people working in them. In the front line of its distribution outwards from the centre, therefore, were 24,000 headteachers, and that is why surveys of over 2,000 of them were included in the research design. When the policy cascaded down into classrooms, however, it was 450,000 teachers who were targeted, so it was at individual teacher level that the application of a national policy of performance management, with accompanying cash rewards, could best be studied.

In earlier chapters the experiences and attitudes of teachers at various stages and in different schools have been analysed and reported. This chapter focuses right down on five teachers, allowing a more fine grain analysis of how the process impacted on individuals. Each of the cases studied is idiosyncratic, so the variety, similarities and contrasts illustrate how a macro policy does not necessarily translate into uniform practice at the micro level. Although both appraisal and performance management were statutory requirements, often with quite specific aims and intended practices, this research has already shown considerable differences in processes and implementation.

Five teachers from the original 32 have been selected to allow closer scrutiny of the varying nature of the performance management process. The selection shows contrasting experiences in primary and secondary schools, among male and female teachers, working in various parts of the country. Different school contexts and management structures, as well as the interplay between varying personalities and their preferences and approaches to performance management, can all help to illuminate, at the personal level, the experiences of those involved. The five teachers and their schools have all been given pseudonyms. They are:

1   Mr Johns, a primary teacher who began with a positive attitude, but became more negative when a different headteacher came to his school.
2   Mr Hargreaves, a secondary teacher who began with a negative attitude, but became more positive when he was given a different team leader.

3   Mrs Rowland, a newly qualified primary teacher, not yet eligible for the higher pay scale, who became socialised into the ways of those who were.

4   Mr Adams, a secondary teacher in a complex relationship with his team leader, a deputy head who was also a member of his department.

5   Mrs Smith, a secondary teacher opposed to performance-related pay, in a school where she felt it was not being applied properly.

Case study 1: Mr Johns – a primary teacher who began with a positive attitude, but became more negative when a different headteacher came to his school

Mr Johns was an experienced classroom practitioner, regarded as effective by his colleagues, who held some management responsibilities and taught in a medium-sized primary school in a small town. When interviewed at the beginning of his performance management procedure, he supported the government's move to make it statutory, but he was worried that it could be 'misused by a less than benign management system' in schools, although he expressed no concerns about his own school.

His headteacher had led a whole day in-house training for performance management which Mr Johns said he had found useful. His team leader for performance management purposes was the head, an arrangement with which Mr Johns was extremely comfortable as they enjoyed a good relationship. He said he regarded the team leader role as 'enabling people to improve, to see what they're good at, to address weaknesses'.

Communication between Mr Johns and his team leader throughout his performance management cycle was regular and comprehensive. The school had provided a framework for teachers considering their objectives. This required them to include one objective related to their own major curriculum area and one in another area of the curriculum, between three and five objectives in total.

At the planning meeting, Mr Johns put forward what he wanted to see as his objectives. He agreed four objectives with his team leader, which included a mix of management, curricular, and classroom teaching targets. The school had prepared a proforma for this purpose. In the left-hand column were listed the objectives. In the right-hand column was a brief explanation of how each could be achieved, with a description of the support needed. The format had been devised to ensure that no teacher was left uncertain about what was required. Once the objectives document had been drawn up, the head returned it to Mr Johns to ensure that he was happy with it. In the event Mr Johns wished to modify slightly the wording of two paragraphs, so this was carried out to his satisfaction.

Classroom observation is a statutory element of the performance management procedure. In Mr Johns' case, his team leader had exceeded the minimum of one observation required, observing him teach on three separate occasions. The schedule used was based on one suggested in the Model Performance Management Policy produced by the DfEE, which suggested the teacher be graded on eight elements. There were four categories along a continuum of perceived effectiveness, starting with the euphemistic *development needed*, and followed by *satisfactory*, *good* and *excellent*. The proforma also provided space for comments on *strengths* and *areas for development*. Mr Johns described the observations as 'Ofsted style', covering 'everything'. Feedback was given by his team leader immediately following each lesson. It lasted around 30 minutes and Mr Johns reported it as comprehensive:

> It was very much, 'How do you feel about the lesson?'; 'Where do you think you should have been better?'; 'What do you think the strengths were?'; 'These are my observations'; 'These are classroom strategy skills, objectives for you to work towards'. And 'Is there any ongoing theme from previous lesson observations? Is there anything that has improved from the previous observations?'

Mr Johns had greatly valued the feedback and felt it was vital that he was observed as part of the performance management procedure. His view of classroom observation was mainly as a morale booster, since he believed that 'everyone should be observed all the time' because 'it builds people up, if done properly'.

An interim review had been undertaken mid-cycle to confirm what he had so far achieved, what was still to be accomplished and to find out if he required any previously unidentified support or resources to achieve all the objectives. He was given some money to employ a classroom assistant, to help with the analysis of pupils' national test data.

Although he had some reservations about pupil performance data being used to assess his effectiveness, he said that:

> ... being on the school's management team I can see that some staff are clearly letting the team down and, without that data ... you actually need that to show someone that 'you're really not up to the mark at the moment, you've got to make more effort'. I support that, if it leads onto increasing someone's skills, rather than being used to knock someone down. And here it's used in a very positive way, but I can see it could be misused, which is why I have the misgivings.

Mr Johns had prepared for his review meeting by considering in detail whether he had met his objectives and identifying evidence to support this. There was initially disagreement over whether one of the objectives had been met, but this was resolved amicably, with the headteacher accepting the teacher's argument:

We argue, but in a very sort of 'debating society' sort of way. There was no animosity with it, 'animated' is probably a better word.

The meeting then continued with the identification of objectives for the next cycle.

Unlike the majority of teachers in the case study sample, Mr Johns had expected from the beginning that performance management would have a positive impact on his classroom practice. He believed that it had done so, but more as an indirect outcome, rather than one directly related to his four objectives. One aspect of his teaching style, of which he had been previously unaware, had been highlighted by his team leader. He commented:

Performance management has probably led to more formal classroom observation than would have happened before and, as a consequence, there have always been points to develop. I had never realised that I did this [the particular aspect of his teaching style], so that was quite useful. In one way it was very trivial, but in another very significant as well.

Mr Johns was a teacher who saw performance management as a very useful tool to help him improve his teaching competence. However, the current head was about to retire and there is evidence from this research, and from our earlier study of teacher appraisal (Wragg *et al.* 1996), that trust and respect between the senior people in a school and the teaching staff, are vital ingredients for performance management to be effective:

I am concerned that, with a new head, everyone will be a lot more defensive and the openness and the honesty that's gone on in the conversations won't be there in the first couple of years. I wouldn't lay myself open to criticism the way I would do with the current head because I know him. I would be a lot more cautious.

This case study represents an example of what looks to be an effective implementation of performance management. The head had made sure that the system was well organised and that appropriate documentation was available for all the various elements of the procedure. Classroom observations, with detailed feedback, and the interim review meeting, had ensured that Stage 2 of the procedure laid down – *monitoring* – was indeed taking place. This enabled an informed and constructive discussion to take place at the review meeting. There was a positive approach on all sides to identifying strengths and dealing with weaknesses, embedded within a culture of trust and support.

All the evidence we collected from different sources suggests that the way performance management was handled in this primary school had helped a committed and enthusiastic staff to continue to improve what they did for the benefit of the pupils. This was what all the participants believed. However, one event, the appointment of a new head, changed Mr Johns' perceptions considerably. By the time he was interviewed on the final occasion at the very end of the research, the head discussed in this study had retired and Mr Johns believed that the new head, in post for six months, had a different vision of performance management. In Mr Johns' opinion, there had been a shift in emphasis from a *professional development* to an *accountability* model. He bemoaned the omission of a personal development target in his new set of objectives and pointed to the emphasis now placed on the gathering of what he saw as 'narrow numerical evidence' to prove pupil progress and worried that those collecting the data would not have 'enough experience of statistics to make reliable use of the data'. He indicated that, as performance indicators were now linked directly to his pay increments, there was 'a danger' that he would 'skew' his teaching to make sure he met the narrow pupil progress targets, rather than taking the more holistic view of his practice that the previous head had adopted. He also believed that he and his colleagues would be much more cautious about asking for help with any problems, in case an acknowledgement of weakness resulted in a lack of pay progression.

This case study illustrates the influential nature of personal relationships within a school. Where aspirations and expectations, for good or ill, are consistent and shared between headteacher and staff, it is likely that the performance management procedure will be perceived to have been effective. Where there is dissonance, as happened when a new headteacher with a different set of aspirations and beliefs arrived, perceptions begin to change as confidence in the new order ebbs. In terms of teachers' attitudes and practices, it hardly matters whether the old head or the new one has a better sense of direction and purpose, what does affect perception and action is whether there is harmony or discord.

Case study 2: Mr Hargreaves – a secondary teacher who began with a negative attitude, but became more positive when he was given a different team leader

Mr Hargreaves was an experienced history teacher at Crawley Park, a mixed comprehensive school for 11–18-year-olds in a large town. At the very beginning of the whole process the headteacher arranged an in-service day for training on performance management and objective setting, and for meetings between teachers and their team leaders. This practice was continued in the following years and it meant that all teachers kept up to date with setting and reviewing their objectives. By the time the research project finished, Crawley Park was into its third cycle of performance management.

Mr Hargreaves had assumed originally that his team leader would be his current line manager, the head of the history department, and when this turned out not to be the case he was disappointed. Team leaders had been assigned to the staff, and although they had been given the option of lodging an objection if they wished, Mr Hargreaves liked his allocated team leader on a personal basis and decided to 'give it a go'. He did not feel that he would get as much benefit from the relationship as he would have done with the head of department and this feeling increased rather than diminished during succeeding years.

Mr Hargreaves was well organised and, at his first objective-setting meeting, seemed to have a reasonably clear idea of the objectives he would like to pursue. He set them out and his team leader accepted and agreed them after a short discussion about the wording. The meeting was brief and friendly, but afterwards Mr Hargreaves said that, although he felt his objectives were worthwhile and the meeting had helped to narrow them down, he did not believe that he gained a great deal from the discussion with his team leader. Comparing it with previous meetings with his head of department, he described it as 'less reflective'. He had hoped to have his strengths recognised, to have the opportunity to share ideas and to have help to prevent him getting stale. After the event he stated that he did not feel he had received much guidance on his teaching or help with his professional development.

By contrast, the team leader, who was also interviewed after the meeting, gave a quite different perspective on the objectives that had been set and on his role as team leader. He admitted that he did not feel he had received enough training about what makes a good, clear objective and that they were all 'feeling their way'. He said he had agreed the objectives, even though he did not think they were very challenging, as they were the ones Mr Hargreaves wanted. He did not believe that his role as team leader was to direct or impose his views, but rather to facilitate the process and support the teacher's own objectives. Neither player appeared to be very satisfied with the meeting, though this had not been made apparent to the researcher at the time.

Although they came from within the same faculty, Mr Hargreaves and his team leader had different specialisms, and after his performance management observation, Mr Hargreaves admitted finding it difficult to cope with taking 'direction from a non-expert'. At the same time, however, he wanted suggestions on how to improve his practice and complained, 'It isn't teaching me anything. I didn't get any suggestions for improvement. It didn't help me to reflect on my practice.' The team leader's comments on the lesson he observed had been complimentary, but Mr Hargreaves already believed himself to be a good teacher, so what he wanted was advice on how to become even better.

The review meeting was conducted in a friendly atmosphere once again. Mr Hargreaves read out his objectives and added 'Done that' after each one. His team leader appeared to accept this affirmation and, using the school's duplicated agenda, asked a few questions about the teacher's strengths and areas for development, resources and training needs. Mr Hargreaves then set out the objectives he had already thought of for the following year. Once these were agreed, with little discussion about specific training needs, he was asked if he was happy with the meeting and passed his notes over to be agreed. Whether it was because complaining to a well-liked colleague is difficult, or because he felt there was nothing more to be achieved, Mr Hargreaves acknowledged all that had been decided. However, after he had left the meeting he told the researcher that he believed another opportunity for professional development had been missed.

His dissatisfaction increased even further after another performance management observation had yielded nothing but praise once again. He said in interview that he really wanted advice and guidance from someone whose knowledge of his field he could respect. Subsequently adjustments to team leader and teacher pairings had to be made because of staff changes, and Mr Hargreaves immediately took the opportunity to ask if he could switch to the person he had wanted originally, the head of the history department. He was able to do this without his former team leader being aware of his request and later he expressed much greater satisfaction with the new arrangement.

The next review and objective-setting meeting was with his new team leader. Once again, Mr Hargreaves had planned his objectives, but this time there was a quite different climate, with a more evenly balanced discussion. As the meeting proceeded the two men built on each other's ideas, sharing a common language and set of precepts. This was, he said in interview, just the kind of creative input that he had sought but not obtained previously. After one particular objective had been fully described and formulated, he said to his new team leader: 'That would be the one for your observation. I'd really welcome an independent voice on that.' They then thought the objectives through, with the team leader suggesting ways they might be tackled and help that might be available, as well as tightening up the actual wording. After the meeting, for the first time, Mr Hargreaves said he felt 'really positive' and believed that the team leader's contribution had been valuable, mainly because of his expertise in the subject matter and pedagogy of history teaching. Towards the end of the period under scrutiny, his earlier scepticism and disappointment had given way to optimism, and he summed up the metamorphosis by saying, 'It's going to improve. My objectives are more focused. I think it will be mutually supportive.'

Despite valuing his team leader's observation and their discussions at the review meeting, however, Mr Hargreaves was still not in favour of many aspects of performance management. He thought it showed a lack of trust in teachers and was 'not a useful way to pass the time'. His assessment of his personal situation may have improved, but his general views on performance-related pay had changed little from the time of its introduction, when he had stated, 'performance management is just the government going round the houses to find ways to pay teachers more. It's another wheeze that will fizzle out'.

This case is an example of the importance of mutual respect in the relationship between a teacher and his team leader, but in a specific context. In order to change what they do teachers must have a conviction that the new strategies they adopt are worth internalising and making more permanent features of their teaching. Secondary subject specialists like Mr Hargreaves place considerable weight on their own subject and pedagogical expertise, so they expect it to be at least matched in those who counsel them, if they are to change the habits of many years. While too polite to be contemptuous of a non-historian, Mr Hargreaves was clearly much more responsive to advice from someone in his own field, which is why the change of team leader suited him so well. Praise from a non-specialist was not soothing to him, as he was unable to convince himself it was founded on expert knowledge of what he was doing. Critical analysis from a fellow specialist, however, was much more persuasive.

Case study 3: Mrs Rowland – a newly qualified primary teacher, not yet eligible for the higher pay scale, who became socialised into the ways of those who were

As she came to the end of her probationary year at Bluebell Lane Primary School, Mrs Rowland was one of a newer generation of teachers who were used to being watched at work in her classroom. Her teaching had been observed and assessed throughout her initial training, while during her first year's teaching she had been watched by the head of her age phase. She had a mentor with whom she could discuss her plans and any problems that arose, so she did not suffer, as some of her older colleagues at Bluebell Lane admitted in interview to doing, from anxiety at having another adult in her classroom. Nor did she think it insulting or showing lack of trust that her teaching should be monitored. Mrs Rowland did not actually *enjoy* an official classroom observation, but she accepted it as an inescapable element of professional life.

Although she was still some years away from being eligible to cross the pay threshold and move to a higher salary scale, Mrs Rowland had attended training with the rest of the staff as she was still subject to the school's performance management programme. This makes her an interesting teacher to study, because the process had begun to make an impact on her thinking when she saw her more experienced colleagues grappling with their applications to cross the threshold:

> It's made me aware, and it's made me analyse where the children were when I took them on in September and where they are now. Sometimes their SATs aren't that good but they have improved in confidence and their approach to work has improved. We've got a number of children with Individual Educational Programmes where the targets have stayed the same throughout the year, which makes you think … I've got to look at that and try to prove what they've done.

In addition, like many younger teachers, she was becoming socialised into thinking in terms of amassing her own evidence. She had started building up a portfolio, even though, as she explained with a rueful laugh, by the time she was experienced enough to apply to cross the threshold, she expected the system would have changed again.

At the beginning of the process, before the staff had received any training about performance management, Mrs Rowland felt she knew very little about it. She assumed that she would probably be observed by the head, who would automatically be her team leader, though in the event this guess was incorrect, as she was assigned to a senior teacher instead. She hoped that performance management would enable her to receive encouragement and advice, but she was less enthusiastic about performance-related pay, because she thought it was hard to measure what individual teachers had done, and therefore unfair to reward or penalise them on that basis.

The head of Bluebell Lane Primary School had arranged for all meetings with team leaders to take place during an in-service day in order to ensure that everyone knew what was involved and could give the process proper time. It was also to avoid the logistical problems of arranging cover for teachers to attend meetings. The head was new to the school, so he had opted for the longer eighteen-month cycle of performance management, believing this would give everyone more time to establish the system and would lessen the pressure on teachers. For Mrs Rowland this caused some difficulty, however, because the objectives she set while teaching one cohort of children did not fit so well later in the cycle with the needs of a new class. One objective, for example, related to improving children's writing and was founded on her experience with one class. By the following November, when she had a new class, she had realised that the context had now changed dramatically, so the previous year's aspirations no longer made sense:

> This year the children are that bit poorer and I think that objective is a bit unrealistic. I think that the objective's going to either have to be rephrased to allow for that difference, which I think will be possible from what I know, or it's going to have to be reworded as a new target for this academic year looking at this class. Because obviously the performance management can only go on the children I'm working with.

This type of difficulty was more likely to be encountered in primary than in secondary schools, where teachers often have more continuity with the children they teach from one year to the next. To a large extent it was a temporary difficulty brought about by the school adopting an eighteen-month cycle that straddled two school years. It was the sort of problem that should be sorted out once the school had got into an annual cycle of objective setting and review. There was a further complication, however. Bluebell Lane had a considerable turnover of pupils, a factor which the head had identified as causing particular problems for the assessment of pupil progress. For this reason, setting any objectives that were tied specifically to raising the attainment of a particular group of children would always be problematic.

By the time of the next review meeting, many of them would have been replaced by other children with different needs and starting points.

Mrs Rowland was very positive in the first cycle about her relationship with her team leader and about the observations and their meetings. Bluebell Lane was a large primary school and there were several people acting as team leaders for the performance management process. She felt lucky that she had been assigned to the person she herself had wanted. Before the first meeting, she had done some preparation, thinking through her strengths and weaknesses and identifying the specific aspects of her teaching she wanted to work on. She chose her objectives and these were clarified at a meeting during which she and her team leader also ensured that they fitted in with the school's development plan. They discussed her training needs and found a relevant course for her to attend. After the meeting she said she was pleased with how it had gone.

At the meeting, a date was fixed for the performance management observation and the focus was agreed, which pleased Mrs Rowland, as it did not concentrate on too many aspects of teaching, or give excessive weight to pupils' behaviour, something about which she would have been apprehensive:

> I was conscious of the fact that I didn't want her to take in everything when she came to observe me. I mean, things like behaviour are an issue here. They were mentioned but they weren't focused on, so the overall focus was kept.

The feedback she received was positive in tone, and she felt reassured that she was achieving her objectives.

A year later, with a different class from a different age group, Mrs Rowland had become more sceptical. She approached objective setting in the second performance management cycle in a more critical frame of mind. Discussing her new objectives, she expressed dissatisfaction at the lack of clarity, even though she believed she had achieved the original aims, as she had understood them:

> I felt I wanted a more measurable target as the past targets were a bit misleading and unmeasurable … although the targets were set there was still no further information on how the targets were to be reached and no indication of extra support or actual timetabled non-contact to fulfil the targets. I have received a copy of the targets which has been signed but still no set dates or guidance have been offered for achieving them.

Her feelings about performance management itself had also become noticeably less positive. Asked about the implementation of performance management in her own school, she expressed reservations, saying that the process had been mechanical, rather than incisive:

We've just kind of followed it through, but there's been no depth to it and no clear understanding on why and certainly no clear direction on what happens as a result of it. I think in theory it could work. It could be a good thing.

She said she believed that it had made an impact on her classroom teaching, but her description of this perceived impact was not on the quality of her teaching at all, much more on her data collecting and recording practices:

I did a lot of assessment when I first got my class so that I was aware of where they were at, and it's also made me log a lot more things about what I'm doing, even if I don't think they're particularly related to my objectives. So I've started a new portfolio just for this year, because I decided I needed to break my portfolio up into dates and years, so I'm much more conscious of that.

As time elapsed Mrs Rowland became more ambivalent about performance management. The trusting compliance of the newcomer began to give way to doubts and uncertainties. She valued feedback from observations and the chance to discuss her practice with a senior colleague and she was aware of the importance of assessing where her children started from, but she was unhappy about the link between performance and pay. Her final comment, during the last interview conducted with her, offered no clear decision about the overall effectiveness of performance management:

Part of me thinks it's just going to be another hoop that we have to jump through, and part of me hopes that the idea of it will actually take off.

New teachers were not yet eligible for access to the upper pay scale, but their progression up the normal incremental scale was still subject to annual review. This meant that they were not immune to the performance management system and its demands. Even before they can be considered for the upper pay scale, newcomers like Mrs Rowland learn the ways and adopt the practices of their colleagues, so that, by the time they are eligible, they can be absorbed seamlessly into the process.

Case study 4: Mr Adams – a secondary teacher in a complex relationship with his team leader, a deputy head who was also a member of his department

Mr Adams held a middle management post as head of department in a large over-subscribed secondary school which achieved high standards at GCSE and A level. His team leader was his line manager, one of the school's deputy heads. In their normal working relationship the two men met fortnightly to discuss matters relating to Mr Adams' curriculum area, and therefore knew each other well. Mr Adams expressed himself as 'happy' with his team leader for performance management purposes. The relationship was slightly odd, because the deputy head was his official line manager in the school hierarchy, but was also his subordinate, as he taught within the subject area for which Mr Adams was head of department. This unusual reciprocal relationship meant he had direct experience both of his appraisee's managerial performance and classroom practice. This knowledge affected the way he steered the setting of Mr Adams' objectives.

When first interviewed at the very beginning, before his performance management had started, Mr Adams said he believed that the process would make teachers think more deeply about their teaching and whether they were doing their pupils 'justice'. He personally hoped it would 'bring into sharper focus my own performance', reporting that his classroom practice had already been affected in recent years by the school's analysis of exam results. The preparation of 'value added' data, and the subsequent comparisons between different departments in the school, had made him 'much more clinical' in his approach to student performance, but he disliked the culture by which schools were becoming, in his opinion, no more than 'exam factories'. When asked how he viewed being observed as part of performance management, he said, 'I welcome it. No-one has clinically observed my lessons and given me feedback before.'

When the first stage of Mr Adams' procedure, the planning meeting, took place, teachers in the school had already been given a preparatory briefing by the head about what this meeting should entail. It was to cover the identification of objectives, the timescale for meeting them, and the success criteria by which they would be measured. This initial meeting took place in the deputy head's room. Both sat on easy chairs away from the desk at a right angle to each other. The deputy head was quite prescriptive, seeking to flesh out objectives that he believed would be appropriate for Mr Adams.

When interviewed afterwards, the deputy head felt the meeting had gone well, and that he had realised his own aims in the agenda setting, saying: 'Mr Adams is a good professional. It could be difficult if someone doesn't accept the issues which need to be addressed.' Mr Adams said he was pleased at the way his team leader had helped him to structure his ideas on objectives, but he was unhappy that he had been given a management objective which he did not wish to have, since his own prime aspiration was to improve his teaching skills:

> I didn't want the management one. The head had said the objectives should be classroom based. But then I am head of department. I didn't want management. I said at the beginning that it was mostly classroom based ... I did voice that. In the end I got two classroom and one management and, as I'm head of department, I thought I had to accept.

Stage 2 of the procedure, *monitoring*, was never formally carried out. No observation of Mr Adams' classroom performance ever took place, even though the headteacher, when interviewed, had said:

> Everyone in the school has one period a week for performance management, either to observe or to be observed. So that gives the process the evidence that's needed.

Before his review meeting Mr Adams said that he had misplaced all the documentation relating to his performance management, so he had to ask his team leader, the deputy head, for a copy of it the evening before the meeting took place. The meeting opened with the team leader making Mr Adams aware of the link between performance and future pay increments:

> First, I'll make a general point – how this relates to the second threshold. This (your performance management procedure) is one of the criteria. We want people to look at this when looking at the second threshold. So what we do today is linked to your second threshold. So let's look at the objectives …

The first part of the meeting dealt with the objectives and the extent to which Mr Adams had met them. He was praised for meeting one of them, but his public examination target had to be deferred until the results were known, and the team leader agreed that there were particular circumstances which had inhibited the achievement of the management objective. In this first section of the meeting, the deputy head used very positive language and praised frequently, concluding with:

> It's worth me saying, when I write this up, that Ofsted says the department is excellent and you, as a curriculum co-ordinator and teacher and manager, too!

Mr Adams initially responded in a relaxed manner to the discussion and seemed pleased with the appreciation being expressed. But once the talk turned to setting new objectives, there was a noticeable change in the atmosphere. It soon became apparent that he felt he was being pushed into accepting targets with which he was not in full agreement. His response was a mixture of near silence and very clear non-verbal messages. He effectively withdrew from the discussion, both physically and verbally, sitting further back in his chair, avoiding eye contact, responding more briefly, or merely saying, 'mmm', as the extract below reveals:

Team Leader: Personal objective?
Mr Adams: Improve IT skills – I can wordprocess but …
Team Leader: Use in the classroom?

Mr Adams:	I'm not convinced it's good practice.
Team Leader:	Well, it might be worth looking at an interactive whiteboard. I'm just wondering … If you have the technology, you can use it and get us [other staff within the department] to use it. I saw it in use. It's very good. You can plug the laptop in … I just think it might be worth consideration.
Mr Adams:	Mmm.
Team Leader:	So we'll put 'investigate use of interactive whiteboard'? And 'greater use of IT in your work'?
Mr Adams:	Mmm. OK.
Team Leader:	And what about developing a website? [Refers to other schools' websites he's seen.]
Mr Adams:	[Doesn't comment.]
Team Leader:	Have a look at their website?
Mr Adams:	I'll have a look. But if *I* don't do it, it won't get done and my time is …
Team Leader:	Yes, but it's such a good website …
Mr Adams:	[Doesn't comment.]

At the end of the meeting, the team leader went through what had been agreed as the new objectives. By this time the Information Technology objective had been extended to include a scheme of work for its use throughout the department. When interviewed immediately after the meeting, Mr Adams expressed unhappiness with the way the meeting had gone:

> I feel I've had quite a lot of work imposed on me. The IT objective, in particular.

He commented that he felt it had been 'an opportunity for praise, but I didn't feel I got any'. Clearly the discussion of the new objectives had coloured his perception of the meeting to such an extent that he seemed unaware of the positive comments which had been made by his team leader at the beginning. He was aware that he had become less involved in the meeting: 'I just got tired as the workload was growing before my eyes.' He indicated that when he received the record of the meeting, he intended to renegotiate the objectives, particularly the Information Technology one, which he had expected to be a personal target rather than something for the whole department.

In the event he decided to try to speak to his team leader before the notes of the meeting had been typed up. When told that the documentation had already been prepared and was on its way to him, he still took the opportunity to apprise the team leader of his concerns. It was suggested that Mr Adams should read the document through and come back if he was still unhappy, so that is what he did:

> ... the document was a lot better than our discussions. There was no setting up the website or scheme of work, just the development of personal IT skills and use of the whiteboard within the 'area', which would not necessarily mean me using it, just me supervising that it was in use.

Mr Adams was still not entirely happy with the objective related to his management responsibilities and, after further discussion, was also able to renegotiate this. When interviewed again, he said he was pleased his concerns had been addressed.

The team leader, interviewed a week after the review meeting, said that he thought Mr Adams had:

> ... largely, felt quite happy with [the outcomes of the meeting]. He was a bit concerned about some of the objectives ... I have changed them. I have made them softer. I haven't said 'No'. I have agreed with his suggestions, which weren't too unreasonable and that is what I have now returned to him for his signature which will then go to the head.

The case of Mr Adams reveals a complex nexus of events and circumstances, a curious superior–subordinate–superior relationship. As a teacher in the same subject area the deputy head was able to apply pressure to his own head of department to venture further into using modern technology. But as a deputy head he was aware there was now an increasing element of patronage, as performance management became ever more closely linked to pay:

> I suppose the danger now is that the system is more and more linked with pay so ... when we started last year, we actually opened with 'this is not linked to pay', but it *is* now, and he knows that, and I know that, although I know that it isn't the only piece of evidence to be used, but it is actually in the government guidelines, you see.

This case study offers an interesting insight into the way in which the relationship between team leader and teacher may operate within the performance management system. These two people were used to working together closely and regularly on other matters within the school. Although the team leader thought he had clearly identified a number of areas for development within Mr Adams' practice, some of these were inextricably linked with his own aspirations as a subordinate in the same department. It appears that an unwillingness to threaten their effective working relationship, together with sensitivity about the introduction of the link between performance and pay, eventually caused him to dilute his demands of his colleague.

Case study 5: Mrs Smith – a secondary teacher opposed to performance-related pay, in a school where she felt it was not being applied properly

Mrs Smith was working in a large secondary school when the performance management procedure was first introduced into schools. Although the school where she worked had designated a senior member of staff to be responsible for performance management and its implementation, the process did not take shape quickly in this particular school. Mrs Smith's attitude was one of cynicism and her approach to the process was influenced by her overall concern that it would be directly linked to pay, something to which she was opposed. In interview she expressed criticism of the reasons for its introduction, fearing that it was another means by which teachers would be given a more difficult time, with an increased workload adding to the stress on them, but it would not put money and resources into areas she thought really mattered.

Her approach to the process was strongly influenced by her inability, and indeed unwillingness, to identify any advantages in it. She saw it more as a 'paper exercise' than something that was going to be of real benefit to pupils and teachers. Her preparation and understanding of the process and its introduction into the school was not helped by the training she received, which she dismissed as 'crap'. The guidance provided by the school did not clarify issues for her and was described as 'a complete mess … It's not clear what channels there are to revise it. We do have a policy, but I don't know what it is'.

Her stated aim was to go through the process with as little input as possible, so she adopted an approach which was mainly passive, neither overtly proactive nor reactive. Although the school did have a written policy available, which was later revised, she did not know what this included and made no effort to find out. Her prime intention was to avoid any unnecessary stress and, as she thought it was unlikely to affect her classroom practice, there seemed little point in pursuing its implementation.

When Mrs Smith was interviewed a year after this initial encounter, the process in her school had still not moved forward. Mrs Smith had not had a planning meeting, had not been observed, and had not been approached by her team leader. She was not even convinced that the person who was her team leader knew of this responsibility. Such lack of clarity helps partially to explain why Mrs Smith was yet to have a planning meeting, but she herself attributed it to the school's general disorganisation and her own laissez-faire approach. She was content to sit back and wait and had no desire to be involved in any part of the process, assuming that 'if I don't do it, it will go away', a fine example of a defence mechanism at work.

As a consequence, one full year after various required events had taken place in other schools, Mrs Smith had still not set any objectives, nor had she seen any documentation regarding her progress during the year. She was not aware whether any pupil performance data were being gathered in relation to her performance management procedure but believed that, if they were, their use would not sit easily within what she believed should be a professional development model of performance management.

Mrs Smith had conflicting feelings about the process overall. She was not clear whether it was meant to be a developmental or an appraisal tool, thereby causing a conflict as to whether it should focus on an area for development, or on one of strength. Although she did not see the school as efficient, nor did she see the management as devious: 'I'm not clear it's about improving performance, because it could be used to judge me if I applied for an internal promotion. I think I do believe it isn't our management's intent, by and large.'

The link between performance management and pay was hazy in her mind at this stage in the process. Mrs Smith felt that other teachers in the school were not aware that further pay increments would be related to the outcomes of the performance management procedure, although she felt that teachers probably had their suspicions that this might be the case. Mrs Smith felt that any link to pay would affect how teachers selected their objectives in the future and that they would opt for objectives which would show 'value added'.

A further year into the process, over two years after the performance management procedure had been introduced, Mrs Smith was interviewed again, at a time when many teachers were into their second or even third cycle. Mrs Smith, on the other hand, was still marooned in the first cycle. At this time she had only ever had one meeting on performance management. She remained disinterested in the process and had sustained her laissez-faire approach. Although, at some point during the past year certain objectives had been identified during her solitary meeting on performance management, she admitted that they had never been spoken about subsequently, so she struggled to remember what they were.

This lack of reflection meant it was difficult for her to comment on whether she was doing anything different as a consequence. Her inability to recall all her objectives meant that she was not aware of any constraints preventing her from meeting them. She had not focused on them and had neither sought, nor been offered, any support in helping her to achieve them. Her views on performance data being used to assess teacher effectiveness remained relatively unchanged:

> It seems to me, because of a bunch of other factors, that it is out of my control. To judge me on pupils' personal life, equipment, time. It shifts the focus onto those two things that are measurable. I don't see all of my job [to be] about improving pupil performance, so [I have] succeeded. They [performance data] don't show up improved communication skills, because they are not measurable ...

Given a process that had barely got off the ground, it was unsurprising that Mrs Smith felt it had had no impact on her classroom practice. Neither she nor anyone else in her school had provided any impetus for her performance management to progress and she had little desire to take action to pursue what developments had taken or should have taken place: 'I'm vaguely aware of something in my pigeon hole. Something in the structure that alerts me to the fact that something is going on – only vaguely aware.'

Her views on the process and on the management of it within her school did not change significantly over the three years our study covered, and although she was not averse to receiving the financial rewards afforded, her dislike of the link to pay and her principles remained unchanged:

> [I'm] happy to be paid more, but I think it's bonkers. It's meaningless here, which accords with my belief – it suits me.

She recognised that nothing much had happened and when asked at the conclusion of the period how she felt the process had gone she commented, 'Non-existently, scarcely, briefly, non-effectively, but I don't mind.' Her criticism of the way in which the school had handled the process continued. Overall Mrs Smith said she was not opposed to receiving advice on her teaching in principle, but she felt:

> … contemptuous of the senior management team, critical of them coming and seeing me, as they don't do their jobs properly. If they were held to account I might be positive about the process. If someone is doing a crap job and comes and advises me, it's a hugely negative experience. More time, paperwork, forms, one more thing to add to the workload if we're doing it.

Unlike other teachers described above Mrs Smith's detachment was compounded by the general lack of commitment to performance management in her school. Her defence mechanism, which consisted principally of ignoring it and hoping it would one day disappear, was reinforced by the absence of any person attempting to dismantle it and secure her enthusiastic support.

All the cases described above emphasise the central importance of context in the matter of performance-related pay. The climate within a school or department, the relationships between key players, and the predominant culture of the whole organisation and management exert a strong influence on the attitudes and behaviour of participants. Paying teachers more money, both as a reward for perceived competence and as a stimulus to change their practice for the better, is a delicate matter. Unscrambling deeply laid down patterns of teaching is not achieved by exhortation, but rather by persuasion and through mutual respect, qualities that were sometimes present and sometimes conspicuously absent in the five cases described in this chapter.

9 Paying for performance

It is unusual for a whole country the size of England to witness the imposition of a performance-related pay scheme within a short period of time, such as happened from 2000 onwards. This research project was able to scrutinise closely and document the programme as experienced by participants at every level: classroom, school, regional and national. Although the scheme was meant to be introduced uniformly across 24,000 primary and secondary schools, its actual implementation was as irregular and varied as schools, heads and teachers themselves.

There are two sets of issues, one generic, the other specific, to be explored in the light of this research. The first is the nature and impact of the particular version of performance-related pay introduced in England, which we studied during the first three years of its implementation. The second is the general matter of paying teachers extra according to their performance.

The performance-related pay scheme in England

The framework – a command structure for uniformity

As described earlier in this book, the introduction of performance-related pay in England in 2000 came at a time when the nature of national and local organisation and control of education had changed dramatically, compared with a decade or so earlier. The pattern of local control, which had predominated throughout most of the twentieth century, had given way to much greater central direction by the end of the 1980s.

Until the mid-1980s this strong tradition of *localism*, whereby schools devised their own curricula, under the somewhat variable supervision of local education authorities, was relatively unchallenged. The introduction of a national curriculum and testing programme, by a Conservative government in the 1988 Education Reform Act, changed the whole system to one where central government exercised much tighter direction of policy and practice that had previously been determined locally. The Labour governments of 1997 and 2001 strengthened this direct control through a series of measures, including the imposition of daily literacy and numeracy hours in primary schools, in which the general content of every few minutes of time was prescribed.

The national pattern of education had thus become dominated by a triangular command structure. At the very top of the triangle was a small but powerful unit, run directly by the prime minister. From this Number 10 Downing Street policy unit a series of initiatives ebbed down to school level. The route flowed through ministers and civil servants directly into schools, sometimes via private agencies. Local education authorities were largely bypassed. Teacher unions became less influential than in earlier times, able to nibble at the edges of a policy, but not influence it as substantially as they might have done formerly.

The introduction of performance-related pay was a prime example of this determined and direct triangular command structure. The scheme was devised and imposed nationally. Private companies were employed to carry out the training of headteachers, while teachers themselves were given no induction, other than what they received from their unions and what trickled down from their headteachers.

Uniformity was intended to be imposed via the training of heads, vital links in the chain of command. This research showed, however, that head-teachers, especially the more experienced, were not always willing to implement policies blindly. Many challenged them, even when the pressure to comply was considerable. The route from prime minister to classroom is not an untrammelled one. It may progress smoothly in the first stages, from the capital city to the gates of 24,000 primary and secondary schools, but thereafter a significant filtering process awaits.

In order to reduce the likelihood of individual variation, the private companies charged with organising and running the induction courses gave all the trainers exactly the same set of overhead projector transparencies to use in their induction sessions. The timing of each of these was prescribed by the minute. One headteacher interviewed during the research said, 'I'm not exaggerating. The man suddenly looked at his watch and said, "Oh my God, it's ten past eleven and I'm only on 10:45".' This style of induction was seen by headteachers as a ludicrous one for professional people and roundly condemned. Questioning the trainers was not encouraged. The very fact that headteachers were expected to be unquestioning, in itself reveals the essentially command style governing the whole operation. Compliance was more important than debate.

Shifting ground rules

When there is strong central direction of an educational initiative, as there was in this case, individual professional judgements become displaced, or reduced in scope, since overarching decisions are made by people outside, rather than inside the profession. A system of performance-related pay is inevitably influenced by the number of people awarded such a bonus.

A *proportion principle* applies here. Different proportions of successful and unsuccessful applicants produce different effects: the greater the percentage of overall successes, the more acute the humiliation suffered by those who fail. If only a few are successful, then good or even excellent performers 'fail' and the reward system fails too in its aim to motivate the workers. A system is only motivational if those subject to it feel they have a good chance of being rewarded. The sense of envy and injustice, however, is shared by the majority, so the collective sense of disappointment can mitigate the impact on individuals. By contrast, when large numbers are successful, the small proportion who fail to obtain an award feel much more isolated, stigmatised and humiliated.

The performance-related pay scheme introduced in England is a good example of this proportion principle at work. In theory, five standards of teaching had to be met if teachers were to progress through the pay threshold and on to the upper pay scale. In practice, the number who actually met these standards was determined by the government, which then passed the message down to schools via the private companies involved in training headteachers.

In Chapter 3 headteachers described the confusion that arose when the information they were given about likely success rates changed during their training. Originally about half of all teachers applying were expected to meet the standards. This was then modified: almost everyone would meet them. In the event 97 per cent of applicants were actually successful. The teachers we studied reflected these changes in their own attitudes. There was much less use of the term 'divisive' by them once they knew they had been successful. Those who failed to meet the criteria became extremely bitter, some leaving their school, or indeed the profession.

One consequence of the shifting ground rules governing the criteria for deciding whether or not teachers were meritorious, was that the standards, far from being seen as firmly based or absolute, were regarded as pieces of elastic, stretchable by political rather than professional judgements. A system designed to reward the especially meritorious had suddenly been transformed into a general pay rise, with a small number of exclusions. Hence the condemnations of teachers and heads about the amount of bureaucracy involved. Many saw this mass award more as a right, than as a bonus for outstanding performance, and so resented having to apply for it in such detail.

There is, of course, an argument that teachers should have been grateful for a pay rise they would never have gained had it not been seen as subject to performance assessment. Other public sector workers filing for a salary increase at a similar level could be told that only those teachers with high performance had been rewarded. These are political, rather than professional matters, however, which do not always strike a chord with teachers themselves. Most of the ones in this sample, successful or unsuccessful, saw it as a mass pay rise and did not like the idea of filling in forms for what they regarded as their due.

Social relations among teachers

There are certain aspects of the predominant social climate to be found among teachers in many schools in England that are germane to this research. First of all, they tend to value *collegiality* more than *competition*. In interview teachers were quick to point out that they did not want to work competitively against their colleagues in order to compete for a merit award, because they saw themselves as a team, hence the extensive use of the word 'divisive' in the early stages, before it became clear that the vast majority would be successful. In some schools this belief is especially strong.

In a study of Inland Revenue staff by Marsden and French (1998), described in Chapter 2, nearly two-thirds of staff had become less willing to assist their colleagues when put in competition with them for performance-related rewards. There was no sign of that rejection of collegiality in our research and often the reverse was the case. When collegiality was threatened, people would soften, rather than harden. The case study of Mr Adams in Chapter 8 shows how his team leader, the deputy head, dropped his demand for a particular target to be set, when he thought about the link between objectives and pay, not wishing to jeopardise the prospects of his fellow teacher.

A second aspect is the tradition of support for staff that many headteachers claimed was already in place when performance management was introduced. A number felt that their existing forms of professional development were superior to what they were being asked to implement. This was often verified by the teachers in the school, but on other occasions there was a mismatch between heads' and teachers' perceptions. Some heads, for example, claimed that regular observation and appraisal of teachers already took place, but their version of current practice was not endorsed by the teachers interviewed.

A further feature is the preference among many heads and teachers for independence of mind, so they show no inhibition about criticising initiatives with which they disagree. Some teachers felt so hostile to the very idea of performance assessment that they became *principled objectors* to the scheme and refused even to apply. This could be seen as a defence against possible failure by those who suspected they would be unsuccessful, except that 49 out of the sample we studied of 50 principled objectors who swallowed their dissent and applied in the second round, were subsequently successful.

Another relevant point is the *high stakes* nature of headship in a culture where accountability had increased considerably. The head of a primary or secondary school often had to take the blame if something had gone amiss. At the time when performance-related pay was introduced, many heads had resigned before reaching the age of retirement as a result of a poor inspection report, criticism of other kinds, or stating that they were weary of office.

As a consequence headteachers who were new to a school were under strong pressure, sometimes from school governors, parents and the community, to secure rapid improvements. In a previous study we conducted of several hundred teachers alleged to be incompetent (Wragg *et al.* 2000), it was notable that a change of headteacher could provoke allegations of incompetency, usually contested, at which point the teachers concerned would allege that the previous head had been satisfied with their work.

There were certain *new headteacher* effects noted in this research. In Chapter 6 it was shown that newcomers were significantly more enthusiastic about performance-related pay than very experienced heads and were more likely to have teachers on their staff who were thought to be unsuccessful at meeting their objectives. The case study of Mr Johns described in the previous chapter was a typical example of a teacher who felt the ground rules had changed when a new head was appointed, so his attitude to performance-related pay changed from positive to negative. Whether a policy succeeds or fails to win the support of the staff can be influenced strongly by the perceptions, attitudes, values and behaviour of a new leader.

General issues in performance-related pay

A considerable amount of what has been distilled in the research described above applies to performance-related pay generally. Although the details and the style of implementation may differ, the underlying principles and outcomes of remunerating some teachers more generously, if they are thought to be especially competent, are often similar, despite different settings.

Changing teachers' behaviour

One prime objective of performance-related pay is to improve the quality of teaching. Since nobody is perfect, every teacher needs to change judiciously in order to become more effective, however that elusive notion is defined. As was mentioned at the beginning of this book, it is not easy to change the habits that teachers have acquired over many years, especially when the profession consists largely of middle-aged and older practitioners with decades of classroom experience.

If teachers engage in, on average, a thousand or so interpersonal exchanges in a single day, with as little as one second or less in between them (Wragg 1999), then this means millions of rapid transactions spread over a professional lifetime. Since becoming more proficient by following exactly the same patterns of behaviour is a logical impossibility, unpicking deep internal structures laid down over decades becomes a central matter. Yet the sheer intensity of verbal traffic during a lesson means that there is little spare time available to teachers to reflect on, and modify their teaching, while actually doing it.

The options open to those seeking to improve teaching include the following, which can be used separately, or in combination:

- *teaming* – two or more teachers working together on their skills
- *sponsored autonomy* – encouraging teachers to decide their own improvement strategy

- *persuasion* – offering advice that is accepted
- *shaming* – humiliating and embarrassing someone
- *coercion* – the use of power to compel
- *rewarding* – offering promotion, cash payments, praise, privileges.

Performance-related pay is one form of the last of these, usually offered in combination with others, like *teaming* or *persuasion*. How it is implemented will reflect the management style of those in positions of leadership.

The performance management element of the scheme did seem to raise teachers' awareness of what they were doing and gave them welcome opportunities to discuss what professional development they needed. The evidence from this research, however, is that *cash payments* themselves appear not to be influential on people's actual teaching behaviour. Most heads and teachers themselves reported that there was little change. The main differences attributable to actual pay seem to be in personal mood and morale, depending on the individual teacher's success or failure in progressing to higher pay scales.

This is not unimportant, because improvement can be closely related to emotional state, but one of the few changes attributed by teachers themselves to the whole scheme was that they kept more detailed records of their pupils' progress as a result of its introduction, so they would have the information to hand when needed. There were very few instances of teachers being able to identify strategic changes in the way they taught, other than merely setting themselves overall pupil attainment targets. Indeed, a number could not even remember, when asked, what their objectives for improvement were, as other priorities had consumed their attention since they had been set.

This strong focus on outcome, in the form of pupil attainment targets, or management objectives, rather than on actual processes in the classroom, was reinforced by the humble place lesson observation and analysis occupied in the scheme. Only one classroom observation session was required for the performance management element of the programme, and even that was not universally carried out, though many schools used classroom observation more regularly as part of their own procedures within the school. External assessors, to the satisfaction of the teacher unions, were effectively excluded from watching lessons. Their decisions had to be based on a scrutiny of paperwork.

If teachers are to change how they teach, it is difficult to see how this can be achieved without closer scrutiny of the thousands of transactions that take place in lessons every single week. The principle that this should be undertaken in collaboration with others was, on the surface, built into this particular manifestation of performance-related pay, with its pairing of teacher and team leader. In practice, however, the main thrust was more bureaucratic than strategic, as many teachers strove to meet targets and supply paper proof, rather than modify how they taught on the basis of sustained self-analysis.

During the period of its introduction a number of national pupil test scores did in fact improve, but the examination results of 16- and 18-year-olds had gone up steadily for many years beforehand. The scores of 11-year-olds actually plateaued, but again, so far as our research is concerned, this cannot be attributed to the effects of the pay policy. Many teachers stated in interview that what they had done in response to the demands of the scheme, they would have done anyway. This included tactics which they were expected to use because of the pressures produced by published league tables of school test scores, such as 'borderlining', which involves working especially with those pupils whose projected results lie at the boundaries between critical points in the grading scale, in order to push them into a higher band.

Decisions about whether teachers have 'improved', by changing their teaching strategies for the better, depend on the criteria used to determine what constitutes 'improvement', and test scores are but one such measure. There is no supporting evidence for or against the effectiveness of performance-related pay in improving the quality of teaching to be drawn from national outcome measures, as this was not a controlled experiment, so the factors influencing any annual fluctuations cannot readily be identified.

Power relationships and patronage

Power in education in England ebbed and flowed from one source to another during the 1980s and 1990s. Successive legislation, under both Conservative and Labour governments, redistributed power. More control over national policies and the detail of their implementation accrued to the government, as local education authorities found their role diminished. Certain forms of patronage passed to headteachers and school governors, both in terms of control over their own budgets and the appointment of teachers. Local authorities played no formal part in the introduction of performance-related pay, though some voluntarily offered advice and training to headteachers.

The overall control of performance-related pay lay substantially in the hands of the government, which determined the form of it, the numbers of teachers likely to be successful, the nature of the standards to be met and the form of external assessment that had to be employed for monitoring. While the individuals to be rewarded were identified locally, decisions had to be made strictly within the rules and conventions that had been laid down nationally. The levels of the five standards that teachers had to satisfy may have appeared to be decided locally, but the crucial determinant was, in practice, the government's switch from expecting half of teachers to meet them, to almost all teachers being successful. This message was passed down to headteachers through the private companies charged with providing their training.

The relationship between and among the key players and agencies was a complex one. As some headteachers pointed out in interview, they were empowered to make decisions about giving sizeable payments to teachers as an inducement to come and teach in their school, or in recognition of extra duties, but they were subject to external scrutiny over these financial decisions related to competence. In practice, however, there was only an infinitesimal level of disagreement between external assessors and heads, each party being anxious not to provoke conflict with the other.

At school level the implementation of performance-related pay closely mirrored the management style operative in the school. Headteachers who were very directive tended to be equally forceful in the way the scheme was administered. This was revealed by the closeness of fit between the teachers' objectives and their own, or the degree of congruence with the school's development plan. One of the case studies described in Chapter 8 showed how Mrs Smith, a secondary teacher in a school with a generally laissez-faire management style, experienced the same lack of structure and purpose when performance-related pay was introduced.

Within schools power relationships hardly seemed to change. Although the role of team leader was designed to introduce an element of collegiality, rather than direct patronage by the head, team leaders were still subject to the predominant style of management that existed already. The intricacy of such relationships inside a school is neatly illustrated by the case study of Mr Adams. As a head of department in a secondary school he was in a fairly senior position and so had power over how the department functioned. The deputy head who acted as his team leader was, in a hierarchical sense, more potent, since he was not only Mr Adams' team leader, but also his direct line manager. Yet he was also a member of his department, so in that respect he was a subordinate.

The elaborate counterpoint described in Chapter 8, during which the deputy head tries to persuade Mr Adams to make greater use of information technology in the subject area, as one of his management objectives, shows the complexity of such relationships, as power flows from one to the other during the dialogue. There is a significantly diffuse boundary between the *de jure* power of the deputy head and the *de facto* potency of Mr Adams, who withdraws from the conversation and subsequently manages to neutralise the objective he dislikes. The deputy head, mindful of the sensitivity of his position as a patron, since he is effectively able to determine his colleague's salary, quietly accedes.

In those schools where there was firm direction, performance management was introduced briskly, with the head taking a strong lead, often opting for the shorter nine-month, rather than the longer eighteen-month cycle. Such schools were sometimes into their third cycle before the less driven schools had completed their first. Changes in the balance of power were most likely to occur under a new head, depending on whether the newcomer sought to acquire it, or distribute it.

Headteachers themselves often stated that they desired more direct power of patronage over merit pay decisions. Teacher unions, on the other hand, were anxious to minimise patronage, hence their favouring of external assessors to monitor heads' decisions. Ultimately, however, it was the government that held the real power over performance-related pay. Once the decision had been made that almost every teacher would be successful, other matters, like the determination of the actual levels of the five standards, fell into place.

Belief and actuality

One problem with soliciting the views and experiences of major players, like heads and teachers, is that there can be a mismatch between the perceptions of different participants. Some headteachers, for example, stated in interview that there was already extensive classroom observation in their school, but certain of their colleagues reported that this was not the case in their experience. It is not easy, especially when there is a strong emotional overlay, to describe a process with great confidence if individual informants' perceptions do not concur.

Various forms of triangulation were used in this research to help overcome these obstacles. *Data triangulation* involved collecting information at different times and from different people, like heads, teachers and team leaders. *Methodological triangulation* was achieved by using interviews, questionnaires and observation and through both quantitative and qualitative approaches. *Investigator triangulation* required all four members of the research team to cross-check interpretations with each other throughout the research, from the time initial interviews were undertaken right up to the writing of the final account. *Theory triangulation* was brought about by adopting no single set of beliefs about the events being studied, but rather grounding interpretations in the light of what was actually witnessed.

Even with these precautions there was still bound to be uncertainty. The beliefs and values of heads and teachers exert a strong conditioning effect on the way they perceive people and processes. Teachers opposed to performance-related pay wanted to believe that it was a waste of time, but even sceptics were sometimes able to point to benefits. Many of those principled objectors who refused even to apply, in the first round, to pass through the threshold to the upper pay scale because of their dislike of the whole procedure, changed their minds and applied in the second round, almost always with success. Some said that they hated doing so, but most persuaded themselves that a pay rise was their just due. It was a time of torment and uncertainty and minds were not always clear when people were asked about what was happening.

Unsuccessful teachers often stated that the headteacher, or the external assessor, or both, had been culpable in some way. This may have been true in certain cases, especially the unusual instance of several teachers in the same school failing to progress, contrary to what happened elsewhere. Obversely, some headteachers complained that unsuccessful teachers in their school had not taken the trouble to give a proper account of themselves. The extremely high level of agreement between heads and external assessors does not offer comfort here, because there were strong social pressures for the two groups to agree.

Researchers cannot make a personal judgement about the rights and wrongs of questionnaire responses from people they have not met, but the intensive case studies conducted over nearly three years revealed that there were indeed examples of people reporting different and sometimes conflicting accounts of what were, in theory, the same events. Belief and actuality can be exceedingly difficult to disentangle in events relating to pay, status and the complex nexus of relationships that are engendered when decisions are made about rewarding teachers for their performance.

Purposes and outcomes

At the beginning of this book we described how the prime purposes of performance-related pay are often stated to be the recruitment, retention and motivation of the workforce, based on the assumption that the best quality employees are attracted to organisations where their ability will be suitably recognised and rewarded. The message to the existing workforce is that good performers are valued, while poor performers are not. Money is assumed to be a prime incentive to work harder. A second major purpose of performance-related pay is said to be the achievement of a closer fit between the goals of employees and the organisation, the skills and behaviour rewarded highlighting what their employer considers to be important.

It is not always possible to link purpose and outcome with any certainty in this research, because so many other factors are at work. In the case of *recruitment*, for example, economic factors can override salary and incentive issues. When the graduate employment market is buoyant it is harder to attract teachers, while during an economic recession recruitment is much easier. The study by Wragg and Wragg (2002) showed that trainee teachers at the end of their course regarded conditions of service and excessive bureaucracy as more important factors than salary. On the other hand, *retention* may have been helped by the scheme, because a number of teachers, including some of the most hostile, mentioned in interview that they were conscious of the need to augment their pension by securing the highest possible terminal salary.

Kessler and Purcell (1991) identified five purposes (1–5 below), and three further ones (6–8 below) are mentioned in a study of performance-related pay in the public sector by the Organisation for Economic Co-operation and Development (1993). Some of these can be commented on in the light of this research:

1   *weakening the power of the unions by making individual rather than collective contracts.* This was not an overt issue, as unions had already been weakened by 1980s legislation. Teacher and headteacher unions were consulted, and the National Union of Teachers took the government

to court in the early stages, but the processes accompanying the policy could not be seen as a deliberate means of curbing them, more a reflection of a state that already existed.

2   *making managers responsible for taking decisions.* Certainly the introduction of performance management was intended to make all schools conscious of the need to appraise what teachers were doing. The principal decision-making on the format of this process, however, was in the hands of the government, while the senior management only had control over local detail.

3   *giving better value for money.* It is not possible to say whether this occurred. Self-scrutiny is time-consuming and it is open to argument whether the time invested was well spent.

4   *advertising the organisation's core values.* This occurred among insiders, though not to the general public, in those schools that made the effort to link teachers' individual objectives with the school's development plan. In other schools there was no deliberate connection of individual and organisational aspirations.

5   *changing the culture of the organisation.* New headteachers were the group most likely to fasten on to this particular purpose. In most other cases the process mirrored the existing culture. A number of schools, however, did introduce a system of performance management where little had existed previously.

6   *encouraging greater accountability.* In the preceding years there had been a shift in education from a high trust/low accountability climate to the polar opposite: low trust and high accountability. Heads and teachers already complained about the large amount of bureaucracy with which they had to contend, so most saw this as an unnecessary addition to their load.

7   *saving money by reducing automatic increments.* Performance management involved an annual review of what had previously been almost automatic: progression up the *basic* incremental scale. It was possible, therefore, to block someone's advance to the next incremental point, but we do not have the evidence about how often this occurred.

8   *enhancing job satisfaction.* The general issue of motivation is an important one. Vroom (1964) postulated an Expectancy Theory, which stated that prospective rewards will motivate employees only if they believe that (a) they can improve their performance by working harder, (b) if they do work harder there is a high probability they will be rewarded, and (c) if the thought of having more money appeals to them. Some teachers in this study stated that they welcomed the interest in them and their professional development, and that they were pleased to have been paid an additional sum of money. Most believed they were working as hard as they could, however, so they saw the money as a right and were muted about its effect on their motivation.

The future of performance-related pay

Irrespective of what happens in any country or region that tries out a performance-related pay experiment the general issues will not go away. As we pointed out at the beginning, the scheme studied in this research was introduced by a Labour government in England at the very time when a Labour administration in Australia was terminating its programme. Attempts to reward teachers differentially according to their perceived competence will continue to be made.

It was argued by Odden and Kelley (1997) that a successful scheme needs the involvement of all the key parties, adequate funding, training, no quotas and persistence. There was mixed success on these criteria in the programme we studied. Some *key parties* were involved, but universal commitment was not secured, as a persistent 60 per cent of headteachers in both our national samples, taken at a two-year interval, were opposed to the policy. Local authorities had to carve out a role, as none had been envisaged for them.

Among the other factors for success identified, *funding* became an issue as time passed. With two-thirds of teachers aged over forty and a 97 per cent success rate, there was a huge bunching at the higher points, with a consequent strain on school budgets. Many schools, faced with other demands on their funds, reached a financial crisis. *Training* was a problem because most heads saw their own induction as mechanical and demeaning and teachers received nothing other than what trickled down to them from their headteacher. *Quotas* were not directly imposed, in terms of a given figure, but the signal was that almost all would succeed, though this generosity began to wane as more and more teachers passed through to higher incremental points. *Persistence* endured for the period we studied, but financial strains began to exert an increasingly negative effect. The government moved from funding all the pay award at the beginning of the process to only paying 30 per cent of the cost three years later. Cordes (1983) discovered that 17 per cent of US school districts which eventually dropped their merit pay plans did so, wholly or partially, for financial reasons.

Some of the teacher unions, when we interviewed their representatives, wanted the programme to be terminated. The National Union of Teachers and the Professional Association of Teachers believed that the process should be abolished. The NUT acknowledged there was one 'silver lining' in that teachers were more aware of what they did. The whole process, however, was described as a 'dog's dinner' which had failed to motivate or retain teachers, was over-bureaucratic and expensive, and it was said that the £125–130m spent on the process would have been better applied in schools or put into teachers' pay packets. The Association of Teachers and Lecturers was content for the procedures and standards to remain the same for the time being, but felt there should be a rigorous evaluation to find good practice and areas where change was required. All the unions were concerned about what they saw as unfairness for non-standard teachers, like part-timers, supply teachers and home tutors.

For the heads, the National Association of Head Teachers was concerned that teachers were being demotivated. The Secondary Heads' Association wanted to see the process of assessment and the standards simplified. They were particularly critical of the one about pupil progress. They also wanted to see a reduction in the bureaucracy.

The research described in this book shows the reality of implementing performance-related pay in all its complexity. Process at classroom and school level can bear little resemblance to the neat orthodoxy of policy flow charts and diagrams. Despite attempts to impose uniformity through training, there was considerable variation in what we saw, varying from enthusiastic adoption to adamant rejection, from carefully sculptured and detailed management of the process to near indifference, with minimal compliance.

The major success of the scheme was in bestowing a significant pay rise on the vast majority of teachers and, in those schools that particularly needed it, introducing a more carefully considered means of clarifying what the school was trying to achieve and whether it was fulfilling its aims. Moreover, the *performance management* element of performance-related pay needs to be considered as an element separate from it. Performance management did seem to make many teachers more aware of what they were doing and how it fitted in with their school's ambitions. Furthermore a number of teachers were able to secure opportunities for dialogue and professional development that might not otherwise have been available.

The most significant failures of the policy may be the limited effect that the offer of additional pay seems to have had on actual classroom practice and teaching strategies, and the lack of success in winning support from the majority of teachers and heads. A related negative factor is the amount of paperwork involved, which was seen by participants to be an unwelcome additional chore, rather than a means to improve practice.

If change for the better is to be brought about, then a fuller and more sophisticated understanding is needed of how teachers lay down, over many years, the deep structures that determine their teaching styles and strategies. One of the significant findings of this research is that the offer of more money alone appears to be insufficient. Interpersonal and social relationships are much more crucial. Even brilliant teachers can improve, but features like mutual respect between teacher and mentor are required if people are to unscramble the habits of a lifetime and redesign significantly the way they teach.

Bibliography

Asch, B. (1990) 'Do incentives matter? The case of Navy recruiters', *Industrial Labour Relations Review*, 43: 89–107.

Barr, A.S. (1961) 'Wisconsin studies of the measurement and prediction of teacher effectiveness', *Journal of Experimental Education*, 30: 5–156.

Bennett, S.N., Wragg, E.C., Carré, C.G. and Carter, D.S.G. (1992) 'A longitudinal study of primary teachers' perceived competence in and concerns about national curriculum implementation', *Research Papers in Education*, 7, 1: 53–78.

Bourne, R. and MacArthur, B. (1970) *The Struggle for Education 1870–1970*, London: Schoolmaster Publishing Company.

Bridges, E.M. (1992) *The Incompetent Teacher: Managerial Responses*, London: Falmer Press.

Chapman, D. and Hutcheson, S. (1982) 'Attrition from teaching careers: a discriminant analysis', *American Educational Research Journal*, 19, 1: 93–105.

Corbett, D. and Wilson, B. (1989) 'Raising the stakes in statewide mandatory minimum competency testing', in J. Hannaway and R. Crowson (eds) *The Politics of Reforming School Administration*, Philadelphia, PA: Falmer Press.

Cordes, C. (1983) 'Research finds little merit in merit pay,' *American Psychological Association Monitor*, 14, 9: 10.

Danielson, C.P. (1996) *Enhancing Professional Practice: A Framework for Teaching*, Alexandria, VA: Association for Supervision and Curriculum Development.

Darling-Hammond, L. (1986) 'A proposal for evaluation in the teaching profession', *Elementary School Journal*, 86: 531–51.

Dean, M.M. (2000) 'Linking teachers' pay to performance is catching on', *Philadelphia Daily News*, 2 October 2000.

Delisio, E.R. (2003) 'Pay for performance: what went wrong in Cincinnati?', *Education World*, 28 January 2003. Online. Available online at http://www.education-world.com/a_issues/issues374b.shtml (accessed 19 May 2003).

DfEE (2000a) *Performance Management in Schools – Model Performance Management Policy*, part of DfEE Performance Management Pack.

DfEE (2000b) *Performance Management in Schools – Performance Management Framework*, DfEE, Ref: DfEE 0051/2000.

DfEE (2000c) 'Threshold assessment application form', part of DfEE Threshold Assessment Application Pack, DfEE 0041/2000.

Digilio, A. (1984) 'When tenure is tyranny', *The Washington Post Review*, 1: 12–14, 12 August.

Dowling, B. and Richardson, R. (1997) 'Evaluating performance-related pay for managers in the NHS', *International Journal of Human Resource Management*, 8, 3: 348–66.

Doyle, W. (1978) 'Paradigms for research into teacher effectiveness', in L.S. Shulman (ed.) *1978 Review of Research in Education*, vol. 5, Itasca, IL: Peacock.

Fernie, S. and Metcalf, D. (1996) 'It's not what you pay it's the way that you pay it: jockeys' pay and performance', *CentrePiece Magazine*, May 1996.

Freiberg, H.J. (1983) 'Consistency: the key to classroom management', *Journal of Education for Teaching*, 9, 1: 1–15.

Freiberg, H.J. and Driscoll, A. (1992) *Universal Teaching Strategies*, Boston: Allyn and Bacon.

Freiberg, H.J., Prokosch, N., Treister, E.S. and Stein, T.A. (1990) 'Turning around five at-risk elementary schools', *Journal of School Effectiveness and School Improvement*, 1, 1: 5–25.

Freiberg, H.J., Stein, T.A. and Parker, G. (1995) 'Discipline referrals in a middle school', *Education and Urban Society*, 24, 1: 421–40.

Furtwengler, C.B. (1994) 'The rise and demise of state-level performance pay programs: a 50-state summary of the reform initiative', paper presented at the Annual Conference of the American Educational Research Association, New Orleans, April.

Gage, N.L. (1978) *The Scientific Basis of the Art of Teaching*, New York: Teachers College Press.

Gage, N.L. (1985) *Hard Gains in the Soft Sciences*, Bloomington, IN: Phi Delta Kappa.

Giaconia, R.M. and Hedges, L.V. (1985) 'Synthesis of teaching effectiveness research', in T. Husen and T.N. Postlethwaite (eds) *The International Encyclopaedia of Education*, 9: 5101–20, Oxford: Pergamon.

Gillborn, D. and Youdell, D. (2000) *Rationing Education: Policy, Practice, Reform and Equity*, Buckingham: Open University Press.

Goldstein, H. (2001) 'Using pupil performance data for judging schools and teachers: scope and limitations', *British Educational Research Journal*, 27, 4: 433–42.

Goodlad, J. (1983) *A Place Called School*, New York: McGraw-Hill.

Gramlich, E. and Koshel, P. (1975) *Educational Performance Contracting*, Washington, DC: Brookings Institution.

Hannaway, J. and Crowson, R. (eds) *The Politics of Reforming School Administration*, Philadelphia, PA: Falmer Press.

Hatry, H.P., Greiner J.M. and Ashford, B.G. (1994) *Issues and Case Studies in Teacher Incentive Plans*, second edition, Washington, DC: Urban Institute Press.

Haynes, G.S. (1996) 'Teacher appraisal: the role of the LEA', unpublished MPhil thesis: University of Exeter.

Heery, E.J. (1996) 'Performance-related pay in local government: a case study of the new industrial relations', PhD thesis, University of London.

Heneman, H.G. and Milanowski, A.T. (1999) 'Teachers attitudes about teacher bonuses under school-based performance award programs', *Journal of Personnel Evaluation in Education*, 12, 4: 327–41.

Heneman, H.G. and Milanowski, A.T. (2002) 'Assessment of teacher reactions to a standards-based teacher evaluation system', unpublished article, an earlier version of which was presented to the Sixteenth Annual Conference of the American

Evaluation Association, 8 November 2002 in Washington, DC, Consortium for Policy Research in Education (CPRE), University of Wisconsin-Madison.

Herzberg, F. (1966) *Work and the Nature of Man*, New York: Crowell Publications.

Hextall, I. and Mahony, P. (1999) 'Modernising the teacher', paper presented at the European Conference on Educational Research, September, Lahti, Finland.

Heywood, J. (1992) 'School Teacher Appraisal', in H. Tomlinson (ed.) *Performance-related Pay in Education*, London: Routledge.

Hinds, D. (1999) 'Praiseworthy reward system', *Times Educational Supplement*, 25 June.

Jacobson, S. (1988) 'The distribution of salary increments and its effect on teacher retention', *Educational Administration Quarterly*, 24: 178–99.

Jacobson, S. (1992) 'Performance-related pay for teachers: the American experience', in H. Tomlinson (ed.) *Performance-related Pay in Education*, London: Routledge.

Jacobson, S. (1995) 'Monetary incentives and the reform of teacher compensation: a persistent organizational dilemma', *International Journal of Educational Reform*, 4, 1: 29–35.

Janofsky, M. (1999) 'For Denver teachers, a pay-for-performance plan', *New York Times*, 10 September.

Johnson, S. (1984) 'Merit pay for teachers: a poor prescription for reform', *Harvard Educational Review*, 54: 175–85.

Johnson, S. (2000) 'Teachers' compensation and school improvement: a review of the literature and a proposal to build capacity', paper prepared for the National Education Association.

Kelley, C. (1998) 'The Kentucky school-based performance award program: school-level effects', *Educational Policy*, 12, 3: 305–24.

Kerchner, C.T. and Elwell, C.L. (2000) 'Paying mindworkers: what is the incentive to teach?', paper based on presentation to the Council for Greater Philadelphia, Teacher Accountability Conference, 16 May 2000, Horsham, Pennsylvania.

Kessler, I. and Purcell, J. (1991) 'Performance-related pay: theory and practice', paper presented at the Tenth Colloquium for the European Group of Organisation Studies, Vienna, July 1991. Oxford, Templeton College: The Oxford Centre for Management Studies.

Kulik, J.A., Kulik, C.-L.C. and Cohen, P.A. (1979) 'A meta-analysis of outcome studies of Keller's personalized system of instruction', *American Psychology*, 34: 307–18.

Kyriacou, C. and Coulthard, M. (2000) 'Undergraduates' views of teaching as a career choice', *Journal of Education for Teaching*, 26, 2: 117–26

Lazear, E. (1999) *Performance Pay and Productivity*, Stanford, CA: Stanford University Research Paper.

Lewis, A.C. (2000) 'Parochialism and performance pay for teachers', *Phi Delta Kappan*, 82, 1: 3–4.

Lindblad, S. and Popkewitz, T. (2001) *Education Governance and Social Integration and Exclusion in Europe* (Final report of the EGSIE Project), Uppsala: Uppsala Press.

Lipsky, D. and Bacharach, S. (1983) 'The single salary schedule vs. merit pay', *NEA Research Memo*, Washington, DC: National Education Association.

Lortie, D. (1975) *Schoolteacher: A Sociological Study*, Chicago: University of Chicago Press.

Marsden, D. (2000) 'Teachers before the threshold', *LSE Discussion Paper 454*, Centre for Economic Performance, London School of Economics.

Marsden, D. and French, S. (1998) *What a Performance: Performance Pay in the Public Sector*, London: Centre for Economic Performance, London School of Economics.

Marsden, D. and Richardson, R. (1994) 'Performing for pay? The effect of "merit pay" on motivation in a public service', *British Journal of Industrial Relations*, 32, 2: 243–62.

Meyer, H.H., Kay, E. and French, J.R.P. (1965) 'Split roles in performance appraisal', *Harvard Business Review*, 43: 123–9.

Murlis, H. (1992) 'Performance-related pay in the context of performance management', in H. Tomlinson (ed.) *Performance Related Pay in Education*, London: Routledge.

Murnane, R.J. and Cohen, D.K. (1986) 'Merit pay and the evaluation problem: why most merit pay plans fail and a few survive,' *Harvard Educational Review*, 56, 1: 1–17.

Murnane, R.J., Singer, J.D., Willet, J.B., Kemple, J.J. and Olsen, R.J. (1991) *Who Will Teach? Policies That Matter*, Cambridge, MA: Harvard University Press.

National Commission on Excellence in Education (1983) *A Nation at Risk: The Imperative for Educational Reform*, Washington, DC: US Government Printing Office.

Odden, A. (2000) 'New and better forms of teacher compensation are possible', *Phi Delta Kappan*, 81, 5: 361–6.

Odden, A. (2003) 'An early assessment of comprehensive teacher compensation change plans', in D. Monk and M. Plecki (eds) *School Finance and Teacher Quality: Exploring the Connections. 2003 Annual Yearbook of the American Education Finance Association*, Philadelphia: Eye on Education.

Odden, A. and Kelley, C. (1997) *Paying Teachers for What They Know and Do*, Thousand Oaks, CA: Corwin Press.

O'Neill, J. (2001) 'Performance management in New Zealand', in J. West-Burnham, I. Bradbury and J. O'Neill (eds) *Performance Management in Schools: How to Lead and Manage Staff for School Improvement*, Harlow: Pearson Education.

Organisation for Economic Co-operation and Development (OECD) (1993) *Private Pay for Public Work: Performance Related Pay for Public Sector Managers*, Paris: OECD.

Ozga, J. (Feb 2003) 'Measuring and managing performance in education', Briefing No. 27, Edinburgh: Centre for Educational Sociology.

Peske, H.G., Liu, E., Kardos, S.M., Kauffman, D., and Johnson, S.M. (2000) 'Envisioning "something different": new teachers' conceptions of a career in teaching', paper presented at the American Educational Research Association Annual Meeting, April, New Orleans. Harvard Graduate School of Education.

Pilcher, J. (2000) 'Educators will watch merit pay closely: teacher merit-pay plan first in U.S.', *Cincinnati Enquirer*, 17 September 2000.

Protsik, J. (1996) 'History of teacher pay and incentive reforms', *Journal of School Leadership*, 6, 3: 265–89.

Reagan, R. (1983) Speech at Seton Hall University, South Orange, New Jersey, May 1983.

Rich, R.W. (1933) *The Training of Teachers in England and Wales during the Nineteenth Century*, Cambridge: Cambridge University Press.

Richardson, R. (1999a) *Performance-related Pay in Schools: An Assessment of the Green Papers*, London: NUT.

Richardson, R. (1999b) *Performance-related Pay in Schools: An Evaluation of the Government's Evidence to the School Teachers' Review Body*, London: National Union of Teachers.

Rothstein, R. (2001) 'Lessons: novel way on teacher pay', *New York Times*, 18 April 2001.

Samph, T. (1976) 'Observer effects in teacher verbal behaviour', *Journal of Educational Psychology*, 68, 6: 736–41.

Snyder, S. (2000) 'Teachers may see big gains in salary', *Philadelphia Enquirer*, 1 October 2000.

Soucek, V. (1995) 'Flexible education and new standards of communicative competence', in J. Kenway (ed.) *Economising Education: The Post-fordist Directions*, Geelong: Deakin University Press.

Steinberg, J. (2000) 'Academic gains pay off for teachers and students', *New York Times*, 1 October 2000.

Taylor, S. (2002) 'Cincinnati pay plan was flawed', *Cincinnati Post*, 17 June 2002. Available online at http://www.cincypost.com/2002/jun/17/guest061702.html (accessed 18 May 2003).

Thompson, K. (2001) 'Performance management in Victoria, Australia', in J. West-Burnham, I. Bradbury and J. O'Neill (eds) (2001) *Performance Management in Schools: How to Lead and Manage Staff for School Improvement*, Harlow: Pearson Education.

Vroom, V. (1964) *Work and Motivation*, New York: Wiley.

West-Burnham, J., Bradbury, I. and O'Neill, J. (eds) (2001) *Performance Management in Schools: How to Lead and Manage Staff for School Improvement*, Harlow: Pearson Education.

Wragg, E.C. (1993) *Primary Teaching Skills*, London: Routledge.

Wragg, E.C. (1999) *An Introduction to Classroom Observation*, second edition, London: Routledge.

Wragg, C.M. and Wragg, E.C. (2002) 'Staying Power', *Managing Schools Today*, October: 32–5.

Wragg, E.C., Haynes, G.S., Wragg, C.M. and Chamberlin, R.P. (2000) *Failing Teachers?*, London: Routledge.

Wragg, E.C., Wikeley, F.J., Wragg, C.M. and Haynes, G.S. (1996) *Teacher Appraisal Observed*, London: Routledge.

Wragg, E.C., Wragg, C.M., Haynes, G.S. and Chamberlin, R.P. (1998) *Improving Literacy in the Primary School*, London: Routledge.

Index